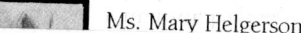

CONNEC†!

FOR INDIVIDUALS AND SMALL GROUPS

CREATING A CULTURE OF RELATIONSHIPS THAT MATTER

BY **PHIL MAYNARD** AND **EDDIE PIPKIN**

Dedication

From Phil

To my amazing wife Becky who is largely responsible for me finding my way back to the Church and a relationship with Jesus.

She has been the glue that has held life together.

AND

To Carol Wood the wonderful District Superintendent from the West District in the Central Texas Conference of the United Methodist Church.

Carol was the inspiration for the content of this book as she challenged me to help her pastors rediscover how to create a culture where relationships matter.

From Eddie

To all the spiritual mentors who have encouraged me on my walk through the years: Doug, Danny, Bob, Phil, and LeeAnn. Thanks for the faith.

TABLE OF CONTENTS

Forward   5

1. Make a Friend   9

2. Love Your Neighbor?   42

3. Circle of Influence   72

4. Engaging the Community   102

5. Connecting Through Service   130

6. Developing a Personal Faith Story   146

Conclusion   162

Appendices   164

End Notes   181

Forward

When it comes to the big E word, we all know how to do it wrong, or how to not do it at all. But do we know how to do it right—with the unchurched, the nones, the never churched, the don't-want-to-be-churched, or the please-leave-us-alone-happily-ever-after-un-churched? How do we share our faith with the somewhat lonely, little bit overworked, slightly empty everyday human beings? How do we even start the conversation?

Does the conversation just start right out where we hit strangers in the face with our faith, so we can fix them? No, of course not. We know better. Somehow that's neither honest nor respectful of their personal space or their personhood. It doesn't honor who we are as Christians, and it doesn't paint the picture of the loving, grace-filled Jesus Christ that we want to share. So, maybe, we stay inside our circle of friends and fellowship in church. And, maybe, we start to find it's easier and more comfortable to stay put there than to venture out of our comfort zones. But new people and new places await. So, how do we start the conversation?

This is the question Phil Maynard and Eddie Pipkin address in *Connect! (For Individuals and Small Groups)*. If you are ready to participate with them in a journey of finding new ways to engage with new people outside your church walls, if you want to help your congregation find genuine and loving ways to share their own personal faith stories with those new people in ways that are life transforming, then this book is for you.

I have not been this excited about a book in a long time. If you have worked with Phil Maynard through some of his previous work, like *Shift*, or *Membership to Discipleship*, you already know that these are more than books, they are rules of engagement with our congregations. Phil introduces us to new processes of self-development, new ways of building relationships, and new ways of being church. He dares us to be bigger than we are.

Now, with the *Connect!* materials, he takes us one step further into the future, and challenges us to go the extra mile . . . all the way out into the far country of never, never land. It's the land where we are so often hesitant to go. But, Jesus is already there, in this land, looking right back at us and speaking so loudly we cannot help but hear Him: "Hey, yoo-hoo, why aren't you over here with me, already?"

In *Connect!*, Phil turns everything we have ever learned about how to do faith sharing upside down. It is not top down information sharing. It is not bottom up catechism learning. It is putting ourselves in the right places for person to person building of relationships, for heart to heart making of new friends, and for soul to soul sharing of our faith journeys. *Connect!* does not preach at us; it journeys with us. Phil Maynard provides the Scriptures, the questions, the tools for an individual, a church team or a whole congregation to self-discover their own pathway to "connect" with those who do not yet know Christ. And this self-discovery takes place in a way that is filled with respect and integrity for each and every person. It allows every individual disciple, each team or church, to find the processes that express who they are as Christians and honor their core values.

Connect! has been the answer to my dream. When I first met Phil at Chili's for lunch in the winter of 2015, I was serving a district of 63 churches that were all struggling to turn from being inward to being outward focused. As the appointed "mission strategist," I was thrilled that the laity and pastors alike were recognizing the cultural shift that has taken place in the last few decades, and they were waking up to the postmodern world. They realized it was no longer a given that people would automatically come into the church. So, this brave laity was ready to take responsibility for the future of their church, and the question on their minds was, "How?" How do we go out? How do we reach the world outside our church doors? How do we begin?

Mr. Leatherwood posed the question to me best at a Pastor-Parish meeting in Dublin, Texas. Their church would be receiving a new pastor, and the committee had already given me their list of qualities needed: a Scriptural preacher, a good visitor, a compassionate counselor. Then Mr. Leatherwood, a delightful and very wise older gentleman, said "You know, we'd really like a pastor who knew how to do evangelism. You know, someone who actually liked to go out and meet new people and let them know about Jesus. Shoot, the pastor doesn't even have to go do that, if they can just teach us how to. It's really our job anyway."

Since then, church after church has asked me, "Could they just teach us how to do that? . . . How do we start the conversation? . . . We know Jesus calls us to share our faith BUT. . . ." We have all met folks who just naturally befriend and engage people everywhere they go and help bring them into a relationship with Christ and the church, but how about the rest of us? Is it something we can learn? Is it something we can do in a way that is genuine and unique to us and our personality and faith?

Connect! says an unqualified, "Yes!" to all these questions. Beginning at our lunch at Chili's, Phil agreed to partner with 15 of our district churches and spend a year of coaching together to answer all these questions. It was a year of discovery. Each church brought a team of five, and we gathered together every three months for a day of learning together. Then, each month, Phil provided the coaching for the experiments each church was conducting. Phil brought the leadership and the passion for sharing the Gospel to this project, as evidenced in the Hospitality section of his book, *Shift.* Phil also brought the mental and verbal clarity to communicate these ideas, and put it together with interactive visual and technical skills.

This became a vivid learning experience for all of us. First, Phil helped church teams find ways to connect with new people in new places by building relationships. Second, he helped each individual on these church teams become ready and comfortable with sharing their own faith story. He gave us lots of questions to help us think about how we wanted to share our faith, and lots of opportunities to practice and try out those stories with each other. Then, later, whenever we were able to connect with someone in a caring relationship, we would also be ready to connect with our faith. There was wonderful coaching throughout this experience. And many exciting new relationships with Christ came out of our year together. Many of those stories are included in the pages of this book.

Connect! taught us that faith sharing is not something we "do unto others" out there. It is something we do with others with Christ. Jesus is already out there in the world, placing the hungering and yearning for a relationship with Him in people's hearts. We have only to join Him as ourselves, offer genuine and caring relationships to others, and connect our faith journeys when He tells us the time is right.

"Come, follow me," Jesus says. *Connect!* helps us discover new ways to do just that.

Rev. Carol Wood
District Superintendent, West District
Central Texas Conference of the United Methodist Church

CHAPTER 1

MAKE A FRIEND

Make a friend, be a friend, bring a friend to Christ.

The above statement is a well-worn saying that many of us have heard in relation to evangelism—evangelism being the introduction of others to the idea that they, too, can have a relationship with Jesus Christ. Following this strategy of making, being, and bringing friends to Jesus seems like it should be such a natural and easy thing to do.

But in a culture in which a mouse-click on our computer or a finger swipe on our smartphone enables us to identify hundreds of people as "friends" (even though we may have never actually met them face-to-face), this process of making friends, being friends, and bringing these new friends to an understanding of how much Christ wants to be in a relationship with them may be more complicated than it looks. Take "Joe," for example. Joe is an engaging and likeable guy. Smart. Outgoing. Lots of friends on Facebook and connections on Twitter. Last year, though, Joe went through a painfully difficult time at his job. The position he held was being eliminated in a restructuring within the company. He would be given the opportunity to apply for a new position, but he wasn't sure he even wanted to pursue it. He was feeling undervalued, unappreciated, and hurt. The years he had spent dedicated to his career felt suddenly meaningless.

To make matters worse, Joe didn't even have anyone with whom he could honestly process what was happening. There were options available to him, of course. He could go to a counselor or hire a professional coach or have a conversation with his pastor. But he realized that there was not one regular person with whom he felt a close enough connection to just vent his feelings—someone he felt truly cared about what was going on in his life.

Joe needed a friend. We all need friends.

Do the following exercise. Imagine that you have been diagnosed with a terminal illness. On the lines below, list the names of 20 individuals with whom you would feel comfortable sharing this news (and all the vulnerability and emotional turmoil involved).

Jane	Lottie	Marva	Jill
Pam	Charlie	Michael	Jessi
Becky	Greg Charlie Marsha		Kate
Beth	Jan	Janet M	Mara
Greg	Crystal	Susan	Jean K.

After you have completed this list, go back and cross out the names of family members, including extended family members.

And after you have crossed out those names, go back and cross out the names of people you know from church.

How many names do you have left? For many of us, the list is pretty short. Some of us have no names left at all. It is a testimony to the paucity of our real friendships and our need to develop deeper connections to the people outside our most intimate circles if we are to fulfill Christ's challenge to carry the Good News into the world.

Of course, the connections we reflexively listed above are people with whom we naturally share DNA (literally and philosophically). To move beyond what is familiar and comfortable and be intentional about inviting others into meaningful relationships, most of us could use a little help.

Our Christian faith is relationship-based at its core, so it makes sense that we could look to our faith families for guidance in the keys to relationship building, but one of the challenges our local congregations face is how to help us develop relationships that count—how to help us fulfill our desire to build authentic connections and learn to be genuine friends—both inside and outside the walls of the church building. And for those of us who are concerned with growing the reach of our faith communities, it is notable that research has shown that if we want people who come to our church to remain involved and active in that church, they need to have developed at least six meaningful friendships in the first six months. [1]

That's a challenge!

There is a sense, as we get to know Jesus, that this business of meaningful relationships is the quintessence of *agape* love (the Greek expression of love in its highest and purest form: unconditional love). Jesus listens. Jesus reaches out to touch and heal. Jesus looks men and women in the eye. Jesus speaks to the real questions of the human heart. It is this expression of God's grace through the humanity of Jesus that separates Christianity from all other forms of religion. God becomes love in human form.

The kind of transformational hospitality in which we extend love to our neighbors through our words and deeds by allowing the Spirit of God to work in and through us is called **Incarnational Hospitality**, and it is the key to producing interpersonal connections that lead others to a deeper understanding of Christ. The *incarnational* part refers to simply being the presence of Christ in someone's life: that is, being a conduit of the love of God to someone else, and allowing that person to witness the power of the Holy Spirit working in and through our lives. As noted, Jesus, himself, provided the most perfect example of what this lifestyle looks like. The Apostle John describes it in these words:

> The Word become flesh and made his dwelling among us. (John 1:14)

The *hospitality* part of this (to use the language of Henri Nouwen) is the act of making room or space for someone in our lives, accepting them as they are, loving them as they are, getting to know them deeply through the sharing of their story, and letting them get to know us deeply through the sharing of our story.

Through developing these skills and providing opportunities for Incarnational Hospitality to happen, the church has great potential for equipping congregations to "be Christ" in people's lives—both in relation to how we interact with those who enter our church building, and perhaps even more importantly, how we interact with those beyond the borders of the church property. This is a thoroughly biblical idea by the way. You are likely already familiar with some of these Scriptures:

- We are therefore Christ's ambassadors, as though God were making his appeal through us. (2 Corinthians 5:20)

- . . . and you will be my witnesses in Jerusalem, Judea, Samaria, and to the ends of the earth. (Acts 1:8)

- My prayer is not for them alone. I pray also for those who will believe in me through their message . . . then the world will know that you sent me and have loved them even as you have loved me. (John 17: 20 & 23)

- You show that you are a letter from Christ, the result of our ministry, written not with ink but with the Spirit of the living God, not on tablets of stone but on tablets of human hearts. (2 Corinthians 3:3)

You might have noticed that there are two significant dimensions—two parallel tracks you might say—that guide this idea of Incarnational Hospitality. First, there is the relationship. We're not talking about a casual, superficial, communicate-through-posts-on-Facebook kind of relationship here. We're talking about a relationship in which we are engaged in people's lives in such a way that God's love is visible. This can take many simple and direct forms. It could

be gathering for a backyard cookout where we just socialize and enjoy one another's company. It could be moms taking turns getting the neighborhood kids to ball practice or just making themselves available to pinch-hit during transportation crises. It might be as uncomplicated as getting together for coffee and sharing life. We might be predisposed to lend a sympathetic ear to someone who needs a thoughtful listener, or we might be willing to take care of the children of a neighbor family in a time of crisis. It could be that our neighbor needs help with lawn care or a home repair or a ride to the doctor. The first rail of Incarnational Hospitality is that of engaging in people's lives in such a way that we naturally communicate God's love just by being sensitive to their needs and sacrificially oriented to help meet those needs.

The second rail is the sharing of the content of the Gospel. And let's be honest, that phrase, "sharing the Gospel," conjures up images that make a lot of people uncomfortable. But maybe for too long we have been making this concept harder than it actually needs to be. While followers of Christ should have a clear understanding of the Gospel message and foundational theological concepts, there is no requirement to be a trained theologian to effectively share the Good News. In fact, that's not what most people are looking for. That is, most people are not looking for erudite theological explanations. Arguably, the most effective sharing of the Gospel message is communicating your own personal experiences, your own story. As expressed by the Apostle Peter:

> Always be prepared to give an answer to everyone who asks you to give the reason for the hope you have. (1 Peter 3:15)

Phil's friend, Bob Allen, is a Congregational Developer for the Rio-Texas Conference, and he shared the following story with Phil that really illustrates the power of unanticipated opportunities to share our faith:

> 'Be prepared for the unexpected' has become my newest mantra. The following occurred on a two-hour flight home. I was already settled into my seat when an elderly woman sat down in my row. We shared a "hello," and I then sank into my seat because I was dead tired from the day's activity. I must have napped for about 20 minutes. When I awoke, there again was that same smiling face. Once again she said, "Hello. What do you do for a living?" And I replied, "I am a life coach." She said, "My life needs coaching—it is totally out of control! I wonder if a coach could give me my hope back? If you were my coach, what would you do with me?" I said, "I would be your guide, helping you to navigate the river of your life and assisting you to examine and explore the great possibilities through a series of questions. I would hope that you would make great discoveries about your life that would lead to new ways to live your life to the fullest. I would help you to reflect on your life and come up with a plan of action."

> "When could we start?" she asked. I replied, "How about now? This is your time. What would you like to focus on?" She said, "I am totally addicted to shopping. I never wear any of the clothes that I buy. They hang in my closets with the tags still attached. I am thousands of dollars in debt on many

" I TRUST CHRIST BECAUSE I KNOW HE IS ALWAYS THERE WHEN I NEED HIM. HE GIVES ME STRENGTH TO OVERCOME MY OBSTACLES AND IS A FRIEND WHEN I NEED HIM."

- KAITLYN, GROESBECK UNITED METHODIST CHURCH

credit cards. All I do is pay the minimum per month, and I am sick about all of this! I need help. I am out of control."

I asked her, "May I respond with a story out of my own life?" She nodded yes, so, I said: "I was a philosophy major in college, and we were told by our professor that he knew that as young adults we were looking for the truth and wanted to get on the right track for living. He told us about Blaise Pascal, a famous French mathematician and philosopher. Pascal put it like this: 'There is a God-shaped vacuum in the heart of every man which cannot be filled by any created thing, but only by God the Creator, made known through Jesus Christ.' If we try to stuff anything but God into that God-shaped hole in our lives, we'll end up dissatisfied, restless, discontent. But fill that God-shaped hole with God and what do we find? In a word: contentment.'"

My new friend blurted out, "That's me. I have a God-shaped vacuum—a hole right in the center of my being. I attended a private religious school as a young girl, and they taught me that God was out to punish me for my sins. My teachers always told me that I was fat and ugly, and that no one in life would ever love me . . . including God." I asked her, "Have you ever heard about grace and God's love and forgiveness?" She replied, "I don't even know what you are talking about."

I spent the next few minutes talking about what my understanding of grace and about God's profound love for all of us. She turned her head away from me and silently wept. In about five minutes she collected herself and said, "Are you telling me the truth? Are you really saying that God loves me even if I have never loved him back? Are you saying that God could forgive me for all of this stupid stuff of buying clothes over and over again? Oh, my God, I have been using clothes as a substitute for God. God help me!"

And I said, "He can and He will if you are open to that."

She looked at me and said, "I have been going to a therapist for over 13 months and have made no progress whatsoever. In one hour with a coach, I have made huge discoveries about myself. So, Coach Bob, what must I do to get on track? I have a ton of clothes in my closet, a huge debt, and a great big hole in my heart. I know that within two days my friend is going to say, 'Let's go clothes shopping so we can feel good about ourselves.'"

I said, "It seems to me that you need to make a plan for yourself. What do you think?" I asked my new client, "What is your plan for what you are going to do if and when your friend calls for you to go clothes shopping?" She replied, "I am going to tell her the truth about my God-shaped vacuum. I don't need any more clothes. I have a whole department store in my own apartment. And then I am going to find a church this coming Sunday and apologize for being absent for 45 years. I need to find a pastor who can tell me about this grace. I need to discover this love that God has for me." She then asked me if God could help her with her credit problems, and I shared with her about Dave Ramsey and how his program repaired the life of my nephew and his wife and helped them overcome their awful indebtedness. I once again pointed her in the direction of a website to explore possible congregations in her local community who participate in a Financial Peace program.

She was in and out of my life just like that. Just a few questions here and there made all the difference in her life. I was given an opportunity to see God in action, and the marvelous things that He can do through me and in spite of me. I now look for coaching opportunities wherever I happen to be at any given moment. Be prepared for the unexpected.

What a powerful story Bob shares, a beautiful illustration of those words from 1 Peter 3: "Always be prepared to give an answer to everyone who asks. . . ."

It's important to note that we are not being directed in this verse to give a defense of the Gospel (what is known in theological circles as apologetics), but to talk about our lives and the hope we have experienced through the Gospel message. There are, of course, many different approaches to evangelism. The following chart will give you an understanding of four major approaches (within which there are many variations):

Impositional	Informational
This is the type of evangelism that is demonstrated in street preaching or handing out tracts. The focus is on sharing the message. It is often seen as impersonal and overbearing.	This type again focuses on the message but is relayed through a more intellectual approach of Christian apologetics. While taking a more logical and fact-oriented approach, it can be seen as too intellectual and even confrontational.
Example: Acts 2:14-21	Example: Acts 17:16-34
Institutional	**Incarnational**
This type of evangelism is demonstrated in invitations given during altar calls in church or at church conferences. The focus is the invitation to commitment as a disciple. While less threatening than other forms, it tends to lack a personal witness/connection.	This type of evangelism is built around personal relationships and engagement in the lives of others. The focus is on seeking opportunities through ongoing friendships to witness to our faith and inviting others to discover God's love for themselves.
Example: John 4:28-30	Example: John 1

The Incarnational Hospitality approach is the one on which we, as authors, will be focused throughout this book. We are part of a church vitality and discipleship ministry called EMC3 (Excellence in Ministry Coaching), and whenever our ministry coaches get together with church leadership teams, the conversation inevitably turns to this type of hospitality. As part of the discussion, we always ask the teams to step back for a moment and ask this question: "Why are we concerned about providing meaningful hospitality in the first place? What are our goals? What are our motivations?" (This is a strategy for kick-starting deep conversations that was popularized by the author Simon Sinek in his book *Start with Why*—an excellent read for leadership teams.) [2]

In the case of congregations that are thoughtful about their reasons for being interested in "effective" hospitality—they usually interpret this as inviting people to come inside their buildings and get involved in their particular brand of worship and ministry offerings—these are frequently the honest answers:

- Our worship attendance is declining, so we need new people.

- We need more givers to support the budget.

- Our sanctuary feels so empty.

- We miss the sounds of young children filling our hallways.

The problem with these types of responses is that is that they are self-serving. These answers are all about meeting our institutional needs, while Incarnational Hospitality doesn't have anything to do with meeting the needs of the institution to which we belong or solving our problems as an organization. Incarnational Hospitality is about meeting the most deep-seated need any human being experiences: the need for a relationship with the One who created us and brings meaning and purpose to life, now and for eternity.

This takes us right back to the quote referenced earlier by Bob Allen, often incorrectly attributed to St. Augustine, but actually authored by the French mathematician and philosopher Blaise Paschal:

> **There is a God-shaped vacuum in the heart of every man which cannot be filled by any created thing, but only by God, the Creator, made known through Jesus.**

The goal then of Incarnational Hospitality is not to meet the needs or desires of the institutional church or even the local congregation, but to fill Paschal's God-shaped vacuum.

It's not about us!

Incarnational Hospitality is not an add-on to our faith journey or something in which only 'specially gifted people' are supposed to engage. Incarnational Hospitality is one of the fundamental responsibilities of every professing disciple of Jesus Christ. The Scriptures don't say:

- "Some of you are Christ's ambassadors," or . . .

- "A chosen few will be my witnesses," or . . .

- "You might or might not be qualified as 'letters' for Christ" (as we read about earlier in 2 Corinthians 3).

We are all called by virtue of our baptism and journey as disciples to engage others in relationships and share our faith. The leadership of the church—in all its denominational varieties—has, throughout history, understood and articulated the need to facilitate this calling. Take, for example, Paragraph 202 from *The United Methodist Book of Discipline*, which describes the "function of the local church" [boldface emphasis added below]:

> The church of Jesus Christ exists in and for the world. It is primarily at the level of the local church that the church encounters the world. The local church is a strategic base from which Christians move out to the structures of society. **The function of the local church, under the guidance of the Holy Spirit, is to help people to accept and confess Jesus Christ as Lord and Savior and to live their daily lives in light of their relationship with God.**
>
> Therefore, the local church is to minister to persons in the community where the church is located, to provide appropriate training and nurture to all, to cooperate in ministry with

other local churches, to defend God's creation and live as an ecologically responsible community, and to participate in the worldwide mission of the church, **as minimal expectations of an authentic church.** [3]

You may have noticed—it's actually pretty hard to miss—that the church exists to make disciples, and that this call to disciple-making includes two distinct phases:

1. To help people accept and confess Jesus Christ as Lord and Savior.

2. To help people live their daily lives in light of their relationship with God (that is, to help them grow as followers of Christ, commonly referred to as disciples).

Read the text below from the seventeenth chapter of the Gospel of John and circle or underline what seem to be key thoughts:

I pray also for those who will believe in me through their [the disciples'] message, that all of them may be one, Father, just as you are in me and I am in you. May they also be in us so that the world may believe that you have sent me. I have given them the glory that you gave me, that they may be one as we are one—I in them and you in me—so that they may be brought to complete unity. Then the world will know you sent me and have loved them even as you have loved me.

—John 17:20-23

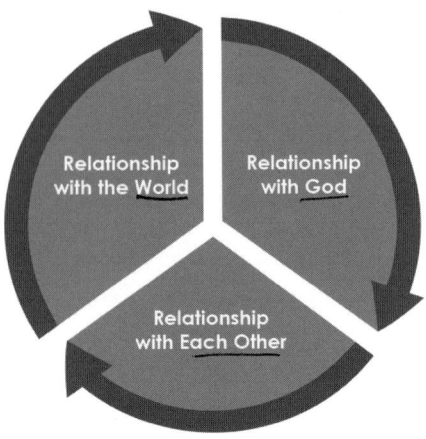

What did you identify as key thoughts?

The graphic image above highlights the following important ideas and the ways in which they are interrelated:

- As we grow in our relationship with God (maturity in discipleship) . . .

- We are led to growth in our relationships with one another (authentic relationships) . . .

- Which lead us to a deepening relationship with the world (engagement with the people God loves) . . .

- Which brings us back to an ever deepening relationship with God (as we experience God at work in the world), beginning the cycle all over again.

So, as we grow in our relationship with God (having embarked on this relationship journey by confessing Jesus as Lord and Savior), we learn how to live life in light of that relationship (maturing as disciples), and this process naturally impacts the way we engage each other and the world around us.

That's the goal.

It follows, therefore, that we should be in active partnership with our local churches and our fellow disciples in pursuit of this goal. They should be the very support system that will equip us with the tools to fully grow and prosper. How then do we develop the specific skills we need to make us effective practitioners of Incarnational Hospitality? A good starting point for you and me, as disciples, is to get comfortable with sharing our own faith journeys. This does not come naturally for most of us, even many of us who have been part of churches our whole lives. Over the course of the next several chapters, many different ways of sharing our story will be presented. Take advantage of them all. Every meeting of a small group or a committee or administrative council or prayer team is an opportunity to help people learn how to share their individual stories and get comfortable doing so. In the context of a safe and encouraging environment (which your local church and the gatherings of your fellow disciples should be), you can encourage other people to practice sharing their stories, while taking advantage of the opportunity to share yours.

In their book, *Get Their Name*, authors Bob Farr, Doug Anderson, and Katy Kotan provide some great strategies for developing a personal witness (the term we church folk commonly use to refer to our individual God-narrative). [4] One of their fun and easy tools for an introduction to this process is called a symbol timeline. The symbol timeline on the next page uses playful illustrations to chart critical developments in the life of a disciple we'll call "Phil."

(handwritten annotations on timeline: "1st born", "5y", "2y", "7L.", "founded church", "xray tech", "Italy", "Turkey")

Here is a more traditional version of Phil's story, using words:

I was the firstborn child (oldest of three sons), which in and of itself explains some of my life perspectives and choices. During my formative years (elementary school) I lived in Italy for five years, then Turkey for two years—the son of an Air Force Senior Master Sergeant. We were then assigned to a base in Florida, and my junior high and high school time was spent there (where the mascot was a scorpion, thus a scorpion's presence on the graphic timeline).

My family were founding members of a local church which started in the living room of a house, then the garage, then moving to a temporary building, and eventually to a multipurpose building. My mother was the church musician and choir director for many years, and my dad served in every capacity except preacher—not to say he didn't do a lot of preaching at home! Every time the church doors were open, we were there. A highlight of this time in my life was participating in a youth choir of 150 members.

After a year of college, I married a wonderful lady—Becky, who is still the love of my life—joined the Army, and trained as an X-ray Technologist and Medic. Following three years in the Army, I left and took a position at a local hospital back in Florida. I also earned a Bachelor's Degree in Radiologic Science. After graduation, I took a position as director of a hospital-based x-ray school in Kansas City. While there, I completed a Master's in Education at the University of Kansas.

This was a difficult time for me. I became convinced that I didn't really need the 'crutch' of church. For two years I played racquetball on Sunday mornings while my wife took the kids to church.

At the end of those two years, I was offered an Instructor position at the University of Central Florida, in the program from which I had graduated. Becky got involved in a local congregation, and she and the pastor eventually convinced me to try church again. I grew deeply in my commitment over the next five years and ended up with a call to ministry. My seminary experience was at Duke University, and then I spent 20 years serving in local congregations throughout Florida.

In 2007, I was invited to join the Florida Conference staff serving as the Director of Congregational Excellence. For the next six years, I supported congregations in the Florida Conference in developing effective ministry. Finally, in 2013, I took an early retirement and now serve through my company, Excellence in Ministry Coaching, where I get to work with congregations representing different denominations all over the United States. God has certainly enlarged my territory!

In the circles on the next page, take a few minutes and build a symbol timeline for your own life. Add more circles if needed. Include both the good and the challenging events. It's OK to use stick figures. Or feel free to fully employ your artistic talents!

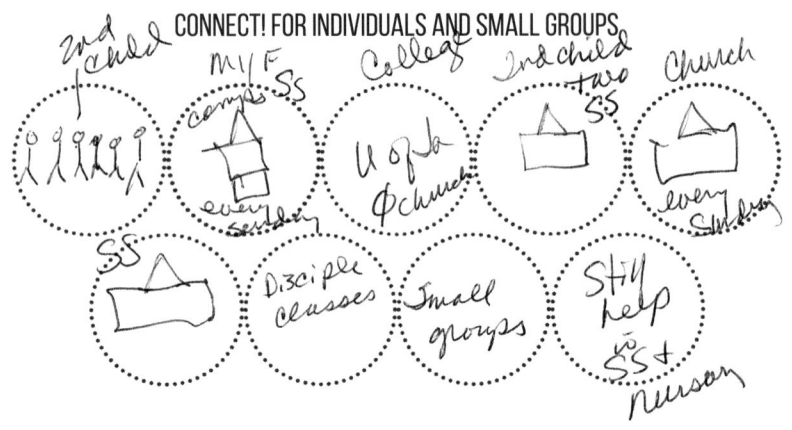

Complete this exercise within the context of your small group if you are working through this material with such a group, inviting each person to share their timeline with the other group members. It will be amazing what you can learn in just a few minutes about people you have known for years. It's also amazing how the power of saying things out loud can affect our own self-understanding. By telling our story to others (particularly by writing it down or telling it aloud repeatedly), we begin to understand our own journey more clearly. We begin to understand ourselves and our relationship with God more authentically.

Such a story is worth telling, and people actually want to hear it (just as much as they long to tell their own story to someone who is eager to listen). So, it's only natural that we start to look for ways to engage more people in potential friendships in order that this sharing has a natural outlet. There are lots of ways to do this, and we aren't called to be geniuses who are inventing new and dazzling ways for humans to encounter one another. We're just being intentional about expanding our relationship circles in the same old ways people have been doing in communities through the ages.

For example, an easy and natural way to help people begin building relationships is to get them connected for a few weeks around an activity of interest to them. Phil tells this story about his first clergy appointment as an Associate Pastor. It was an experience that turned on a light bulb for him regarding the power of simple gatherings to help people make connections. The parsonage provided with this clergy appointment was directly adjacent to the church property (you could even enter into the back gate from the church). It was an ideal place for informal gatherings. Phil's wife, Becky, was asked to host an eight-week series on Mexican cooking, which Phil claims turned out to be just about the best eight weeks of his life. He loves Mexican food. To be clear, she was not the one doing the teaching—they just hosted the group. But each week he would come home to a house filled with the mouth-watering aroma of great Mexican dishes.

Yet, he relates, he was astounded! (He adds some extra theatrics at this point in the story.) Sitting in the library adjacent to the kitchen, he could overhear snippets of conversation, and the participants weren't talking about Mexican dishes. These ladies were talking about their families, their husbands, their jobs, their churches, and even their faith! Didn't they know they were supposed to be talking about Mexican cooking?

Of course, they were talking about other things. That's what happens when we provide the space for relationships to develop. The point here, in case you missed it, is that relationships naturally occur when we make room for them. And significant conversations happen even when the theme is not focused overtly on discipleship.

As we at EMC3 work with churches in developing ways to foster this kind of relational connection, we like to use a limited version of an Asset Mapping Exercise. We give each participant six Post-it notes (this exercise works best with groups of 15 or more) and ask each person to write down three things they are good at—one on each of three Post-it notes. Then we ask them to identify three things they would like to learn how to do or learn how to do better—again, one on each of the three Post-it notes.

It is important to let them know that the things they identify don't have to be churchy things. For example: cooking, organizing, playing guitar, financial management, sewing, quilting, scrapbooking, and investing are all great things. We emphasize, on the other hand, that basic life functions like talking, sleeping, eating, caring, or loving are not the kinds of things we're looking for in this particular exercise. Then we ask participants to place the Post-it notes of things they are good at on one side of a wall or white board, and the things they would like to learn how to do or to do better on the other side.

In the scores of times this exercise has been carried out, it always produces the same result. Within this one room, there are people who are good at things that match up with people who would like to learn how to do those things or learn how to do them better.

So the questions become:

- Would people be blessed if we got the 'good ats' together with 'want to learns"?

- Would new skills be developed?

- Would new relationships be built?

- Would significant conversations happen?

The answer to each of these questions is a resounding yes!

And perhaps we should be asking an even more significant question: If there are this many people within a particular congregation who want to learn how to do this particular skill, how many more might there be in the community around us?

What if we were to announce a meetup.com group around one of the themes identified? Meet up groups are just neighbors getting together to learn something, do something, or share something. Even while writing this, we pulled out a smartphone and did a quick check on all of the possible groups to meet up with in our immediate vicinity. There were 54 different groups registered! Could it make a difference in people's lives, in our communities, and maybe even in our churches if we made room for people to get together and build relationships and share their stories? For some of our churches, space is definitely one resource we have to offer. Why not fill that space with the men, women, and children from the community who are participating in wholesome activities from book groups to fitness classes? Most of us have hobbies and interests beyond our participation in worship and Bible studies. Why not partner with the congregations of which we are a part to provide facilities and support for some of those interests as a way to connect with the unchurched—that is, the-currently-unconnected-to-a-community-of-faith—so that they can get to know us?

There are ideas for how we can independently host get-togethers on our own, and there are ideas for how we can work together in conjunction with our faith families to offer bigger events based through our churches.

Gathering Events

You may find this incredibly difficult to believe, but people outside of the church often have the perspective that church people are boring. They have the false impression that all we do is sit around and read the Bible and talk about Scripture verses, or go to dinners where we're served casseroles and endure monotone lectures about deep theological topics like *predestinationalism*. Maybe we should bear witness to church people being normal, regular folks who like to have as much fun as the next person.

Phil's daughter recently called and invited him and Becky to a 'neighborhood movie event' at her home. They set up a movie screen, a card table, and projector linked to an iPad with a movie downloaded to play—probably involving minions or Disney princesses; Phil can't remember. But he distinctly remembers that the screen was set up in the grass in her front yard close to the street, and people brought their own chairs or blankets. Drinks were provided, and people brought popcorn and cookies to share. All in all, there were about 40 people gathered (about half children) enjoying a kids' movie and conversation.

Low key. Easy. Fun. Relationship building.

There is no limit to the variety of things that can be done as 'gathering events.' For example:

- Participate in planting sea grass to protect the dunes at the beach.

- Hold a 'Biker Sunday' and invite motorcyclists of every stripe to join you for worship, a cook-out, and 'biker games'—be sure to bless the bikes!

- Set up a bouncy house and cook hamburgers to give away to all who come and enter into conversation.

- Set up a parents' morning out at the park and enjoy conversation while the kids play, or the parents could bring the kids to a McDonald's PlayPlace and enjoy refreshments while the kids run through tunnels and leap into ball pits.

- Set up a 'movie in the park' or 'neighborhood flick' and invite anybody you see to join you.

- Invite neighbors and friends to join you for a BBQ in your back yard or just set a BBQ up next to the street with a sign that says 'free food.'

- Have a soccer, flag football, or volleyball game at a local park.

You get the idea!

Connect Groups

Sometimes referred to as affinity groups, these are regular gatherings of people with a common interest. This is one of the easiest ways to get people connected with others and provide space for natural relationships to be built. We mentioned earlier that research focused on congregational vitality indicates that the key to people bonding with a local church community and staying involved long-term is the formation of relationships with at least six people. An individual needs that many relationships to feel genuinely comfortable and connected. Those bonds can grow in all sorts of ways, but among the most powerfully connected are people who are linked by their passions and interests. These kinds of potential affinity groups are almost limitless:

- Cycling
- Biking
- Scrapbooking
- Sewing
- Bowling
- Hiking
- Fishing
- Golfing
- Reading
- Investing

Use your imagination. The key is to have a person who is passionate about the particular interest who can be a facilitator, the glue who is excited about the work of organizing the group and keeping the energy level high. Write down some of you own hobbies and interests:

golf   walking   cooking
tennis   exercise   baking
reading   trips   essential oils

"I CAN'T IMAGINE GOING THROUGH LIFE'S TWISTS AND TURNS WITHOUT THE LOVE OF GOD - STRUGGLING THROUGH THE VALLEYS WITHOUT THE COMPASSION OF THE SON; REACHING THE MOUNTAINTOP WITHOUT CELEBRATING THE POWER OF THE FATHER; OR WATCHING MY FAMILY GROW WITHOUT THE GUIDANCE OF THE HOLY SPIRIT. I CAN'T IMAGINE."

- SUSAN, LINE STREET UNITED METHODIST CHURCH

Which of these are actually activities around which you could build an affinity group?

The discipleship aspect (the second of the two rails we illustrated earlier in the chapter) comes into play as leaders of these groups are intentional about including a few minutes of prayer/Scripture/devotional. This sets their group apart from community organizations like Kiwanis, Rotary, or the gardening club. It also begins to form a bridge to participation in a more focused discipleship group.

Not only do Connect Groups provide space for the building of relationships. They provide space for deeper conversations and reflection. They also witness to the fact that disciples of Jesus are by no means opposed to having a good time.

Community Service Opportunities

Want to help people build strong relationships? Give them opportunities to serve together making a difference in the surrounding community.

Want to help people grow in their relationship with Jesus? Give them opportunities to serve together making a difference in the surrounding community.

Want to witness to those outside the church that the church is relevant and cares about the community? Provide opportunities for all sorts of folks to serve together making a difference in the community.

There's just something about getting people working together to make a difference that builds relationships that go way beyond the service activity itself. Some churches actively support teams for a Relay for Life event (a national event with iterations in local communities that raise money for cancer research). Some walk, others serve refreshments, and still others minister through a 'prayer tent.' It's a great way to have your church sponsor an event, while leaving plenty of opportunities open to include friends, acquaintances, and co-workers to support a fund-raiser or community service activity that they feel good about.

A new church plant started taking teams around the neighborhoods directly surrounding the church property, just picking up trash on Saturday mornings and witnessing to their concern for the community and the world. People asked why they were doing this, and they responded "because we're the church and we care about this community." Pretty soon, non-church people from the surrounding neighborhoods began to join this weekly service project. After a while, there wasn't nearly as much trash to pick up, because others in the area had begun to care as well. What a great initiative to demonstrate the practical ways God has called us to love, and thereby influence, our communities.

Some churches have begun to think creatively about how they can be good stewards and good neighbors by establishing community gardens. Some of the vegetables and fruit go directly to families in need. The rest is used to support the local food pantry, providing fresh vegetables in addition to packaged goods. Many times, even people who are skeptical of theology or past church experiences are motivated to make a difference in tangible ways. Partner with them as a way to establish relationships (and do the kind of good the Gospel calls us to do).

What are the needs and opportunities in your community?

Dinner for Eight

Everybody likes to eat, and most people enjoy getting together for dinner with someone else. Why not help this happen in a way that encourages and supports the building of relationships?

Dinner for eight—or whatever multiplier works well in your setting—is simply four couples getting together for dinner. This can happen in someone's home or at a local restaurant. With just a little support from the church, this can be a great way to connect people together who have found themselves on the fringe of the church or intimidated about how to meet new people. What a great way to facilitate making new friends or convert casual acquaintances to deeper friendships. By rotating hosting households, it's even a great way to get to know more about different neighborhoods.

In many churches that have tried a version of this, it's used as a way to get people within a congregation to know each other better (and is a strong tool for doing so, particularly if the makeup of the dinner groups is shuffled every few months). One way to score a really big win with this format would be to have three couples from the church connecting with a couple from outside the church to introduce them to some great new people. This is a natural process in the sense of inviting along an unchurched couple with whom you have already established a relationship, however casual an acquaintance, so that they can meet other couples for whom faith is a major part of their lives—but making these connections in an atmosphere that is natural and non-threatening.

So effective is this relationship-building strategy that many new church plants use this format to get congregational founders directly connected to those in the community. One of the couples in attendance can be representatives of the leadership of the congregation just in case a question comes up about the church that the others don't know how to answer. This can be a potent growth strategy for churches, because it is a direct pathway to powerful relationships.

Prayer

Last, but certainly not least, as followers of Christ we should never underestimate the power of prayer. It is transformative to be in prayer for the people in our lives who do not yet know how much God loves them.

We love to tell the story of the man—we'll call him Harvey—that we met while doing an on-site consultation with a local congregation. The story of how he came to be involved in church leadership bore inspiring witness to the power of praying for those not yet connected to God. This man described how his wife and her sister had prayed for nearly three years for him to come to know Jesus. He was resistant to their efforts to say the least. That was a solid three years during which he gave them no sign whatsoever that their prayers were having an effect, but still they prayed faithfully. Eventually, though, God's grace broke through, and he is now a leader in this local congregation, attributing his relationship with Jesus to the power of prayers offered on his behalf.

Imagine how transformative it would be if we all made it a spiritual discipline to be in prayer for specific friends, acquaintances, or recognizable strangers whom we sense need a caring or encouraging relationship in their lives? What would happen if we were to get everyone in our congregations to pray specifically for three to four people each year, asking God to open doors for us to be in ministry to them and share our lives and faith stories with them? The lives of those who prayed such prayers would be transformed, not to mention the potential transformation of the lives of those for whom they are praying. Such a church would certainly be living into its mission.

We should encourage our church leadership (or perhaps we are that leadership) to incorporate this vision of targeted prayer as part of the corporate/pastoral prayer offered in worship each weekend. It's not necessary to go through the phone book and start praying for people by name, just that we publicly state the importance of reaching out to the many people in our community who don't know the love of God. We can make it a specific point to pray for an opportunity to be Christ in their lives. And in all of our congregational communications, we can offer challenges to lift people up in prayer, not just for healing or traveling mercies or to find a new job, but that we might be given opportunities by God to show Christ's love to them in tangible ways.

Incarnational Hospitality happens most effectively when we are in relationship with people outside the church, seeking ways to be Christ in their lives and to invite them to discover the abundant, eternal life that is offered to them. It is this carefully nurtured relationship that establishes the credibility and provides the opportunity. It is the sharing of our stories that helps people discover the Good News of Jesus for their own lives.

Connecting with the Millennials

Before we conclude the conversation about making friends—real friends—in the church and beyond, it seems important to share some thoughts about connecting with the generation most congregations seem to be missing in significant numbers: the millennials. This is the distinctive demographic group that is the subject of the most hand wringing at ministry leadership conferences and in the individual coaching sessions on which we consult. The indistinctly defined term millennials is generally used to describe the young people who came of age around the year 2,000. They are sometimes also referred to as Generation Y. [5]

This broad category of young adults is defined by different priorities, life experiences, and expectations than the Baby Boomers. And while they have been saying 'no thanks' to traditional organized religion in statistically significant droves, some congregations have apparently unlocked the key to what engages them. The consensus about why these churches are more successful in connecting to this particular age group (and the generation that follows them) boils down to at least four significant themes.

First, the importance of **authenticity**. This means that people are real with each other. It means we acknowledge that there are things in life we still struggle to overcome or deal with. We're honest about the fact that there are things we don't understand. We celebrate the truth that we're all on this journey together (even church leaders).

Second, the focus on **relevance**. Our faith has to apply to our lives. It has to mean something that impacts the way we do life as individuals and how we do life together. One of the great powers of relationships is that we get to share how we see God at work in our lives.

Third, the value of **individual experiences**. Not everyone's experience of God is going to be the same. One of the powers of authentic community is that we can learn from each other's experiences and accept that they might not be our own.

Fourth, the centrality of **compassion**. This, of course, takes many forms. It may include serving the needy or standing up for the disenfranchised. It may take welcoming someone into our home or accepting someone with a different lifestyle. The key is a relational component that reflects the love of Christ through us.

While these seem to be the major themes that capture the hearts of millennials, they really go beyond the longings of just one group. They certainly capture the spiritual aspirations of the demographic cluster just behind them, the so-called Generation Z. And, if we are honest, they might just capture the longings of all of us who seek to dynamically live out the core values of our relational faith!

MAKE A FRIEND
Questions and Exercises for Individuals

1. Complete the "terminal illness" exercise on page 10. Did you gain any insights about your closest non-family relationships?

   not too many

2. In your own words, write down a definition of Incarnational Hospitality as you understand it.

3. What is the most intimidating challenge of sharing your faith with others?

   timid

4. On page 20, there is a statement that the function of the local church is to make disciples. Think about your own personal participation in the life of your congregation. How do the activities in which you are engaged at your church fulfill this function or equip you to go out into the world and fulfill this function?

5. If you haven't already completed the symbol timeline demonstrated on page 26, do so now. What insights did you gain into your own story? In what ways can such a timeline help you share your faith?

6. If you haven't already listed some hobbies and interests as directed on page 31, turn there and do so now. Can you see yourself helping to organize a group around one of these activities or interests? If not, what's holding you back? Do you have any professional or life skills that might be interesting or useful to share with others? If you could encourage your church to sponsor one new course, activity, or interest group, what would it be?

7. In what ways have you already been involved in community service (beyond ministries sponsored and run by your congregation)? What are some ways of serving in the community that have prompted your interest?

8. In what demographic do you find yourself (Baby Boomer / Gen Xer / Millennial)? Have you noticed differences in the various generations and how they perceive church participation and discipleship? What is most frustrating to you about these differences? What is most exciting? How has your congregation worked to bridge the divide and bring different cultural and demographic groups together to understand each other's unique spiritual insights and ministry strengths?

Discussion and Activities for Small Group Settings

In addition to comparing your individual responses to the questions from the previous pages, as well as the group activities suggested within the chapter, give some thoughts to the more institutionally oriented questions below.

1. Why is it important for the Church to encourage Incarnational Hospitality?

2. What are the 'wins' resulting from successful relationship building and faith sharing?

3. How could your congregation equip people to share their stories?

4. What types of 'relationship building' support are happening in your congregation now? What might be helpful to include?

5. What are some next steps your congregation could take to equip and support the development of incarnational hospitality?

• CHAPTER 2 •

LOVE YOUR NEIGHBOR?

Remember the popular *Cheers* theme song, "Where Everybody Knows Your Name"?

> *Sometimes you want to go*
> *Where everybody knows your name,*
> *And they're always glad you came;*
> *You want to be where you can see*
> *Our troubles are all the same;*
> *You want to be where everybody knows your name.*

Imagine living in a neighborhood where the unsung but implied theme song is exactly the opposite:

> *Nobody wants to go*
> *Where nobody knows your name,*
> *And they couldn't care less if you came;*
> *Nobody wants to be where everyone agrees*
> *That other people's troubles are lame;*
> *Nobody wants to be where nobody knows your name.*

That's a ridiculous set of lyrics, but for many people it's how they feel when they think about their neighbors. For a lot of people—maybe even you, if you're being honest with yourself—the feeling of the kind of welcoming community encountered by the patrons of Cheers is hard to imagine. We pull into the driveway of our home and click the garage door opener, park our car, and close the garage door. Our "porches" are patios or decks on the backside of the house where we don't even have to see our neighbors walk by. The play area for our kids is located in the backyard. We have six-foot high fences to keep the dogs in and the neighbors out.

Or maybe we live in a more rural setting in which it is easy to rarely make actual eye contact with our neighbors. They are just far enough away over the hill or down the road that we give them an occasional wave in passing, or run into them at the local grocery or the library and offer them a perfunctory greeting.

You get the picture. We know they are there—they are perhaps even a recognizable and familiar part of the rhythm of our lives.

By definition—that is, the actual dictionary definition—we are neighbors:

<u>Neighbor</u>

Noun: A person living near or next door to the speaker or person referred to.

Verb: (of a place or thing) be situated next to or very near to.

In *practice*, however, we are strangers.

Truth be told, the way we often talk about neighbors in the church doesn't help very much. Our proof text is the story of the Good Samaritan, a parable that Jesus shared in response to the expert in the law who asked, "And who is my neighbor?"

A man was going down from Jerusalem to Jericho, when he fell into the hands of robbers. They stripped him of his clothes, beat him, and went away leaving him half dead. A priest happened to be going down the same road, and when he saw the man, he passed by on the other side. So too, a Levite, when he came to the place and saw him, passed by on the other side. But a Samaritan, as he traveled, came where the man was; and when he saw him he took pity on him. He went to him and bandaged his wounds, pouring on oil and wine. Then he put the man on his own donkey, brought him to an inn and took care of him. The next day he took out two denarii and gave them to the innkeeper. "Look after him," he said, "and when I return I will reimburse you for any extra expense you may have."

Which of these do you think was a neighbor to the man who fell into the hands of the robbers?

The expert in the law replied, "The one who had mercy on him."

Jesus told him, "Go and do likewise." (Luke 10:25-37)

You've probably heard this text preached dozens of times, in lots of different creative presentations with many different emphases and conclusions.

We could talk about the laws regarding cleanliness in the Jewish tradition.

We could talk about keeping our traditions pure.

We could talk about the outcast being the one who responded with mercy.

We could even talk about generosity and the ability of the Samaritan to be magnanimous because he lived within margins and had available resources to offer in this time of emergency need.

We could talk about "everyone we encounter who needs us" as the person who is our neighbor. But this kind of broad definition is exactly where the practical problem begins. If everyone is our neighbor, it becomes impossible to really be a good neighbor to anyone. Our focus is too diluted, the logistical challenges of being all things neighborly to all people becomes exhausting.

What if, however, we went back to the original question and Jesus' response to it?

On one occasion an expert in the law stood up to test Jesus.

"Teacher," he asked, "what must I do to inherit eternal life?"

"What is written in the Law?" he replied. "How do you read it?"

He answered, "'Love the Lord your God with all your heart and with all your soul and with all your strength and with all your mind,' and 'Love your neighbor as yourself.'"

"You have answered correctly," Jesus replied. (Luke 10:25-28)

Love your neighbor.

What if Jesus really meant that? What if Jesus meant those in our actual neighborhoods? As in the house next door to us? As in the people on our street?

What if we were to flip the opening scenario upside down?

What if . . . instead of sitting on our back porches, we sat out in front of our homes and greeted our neighbors as they walked by with their dogs or while just out for an evening stroll? Or if we live out in the country, what if we made it a point to head down to the crossroads store and have a cup of coffee, intentionally hanging out a while to chat up our neighbors as they pass through?

A friend of mine made it a practice to set up a couple of lawn chairs at the end of the driveway and have some drinks in a cooler. As people came by, he would start up a conversation, offer a cool drink, and invite them to 'sit a spell.' When the weather got colder, he would set up a charcoal grill to provide some warmth. Over a period of weeks, he got to know just about everyone in the neighborhood.

What if . . . instead of having the play area for the kids in the backyard, we located some outdoor toys and sports equipment in the front yard? Imagine the kids from down the street coming over and playing with your kids. And imagine the parents of the kids in the neighborhood coming over to check on their happy, engaged children, and then naturally falling into conversation with you. And if we don't happen to live in a traditional subdivision setting, what if we took some initiative and loaded up some sports balls and toys, along with a couple of packages of cookies and some cold drinks, and we headed to the community park and invited kids and their parents to interact with our families and share our snacks?

What if . . . instead of grilling our dinner out back just for our family, we invited the neighbors over and had a BBQ together?

You get the idea. It's a very literal interpretation of that 'love your neighbor' stuff.

Unfortunately, the daily reality of this go-go-go world is that most of us don't even know our neighbors. In the appendices of this book is an exercise to help us see the reality of this. It is adapted from another book, *Like Your Neighbor* by Stephen Sorenson. [1] Take a few minutes now to go there, complete the exercise, and see what insights are revealed. *p. 168*

LOVE YOUR NEIGHBOR EXERCISE:

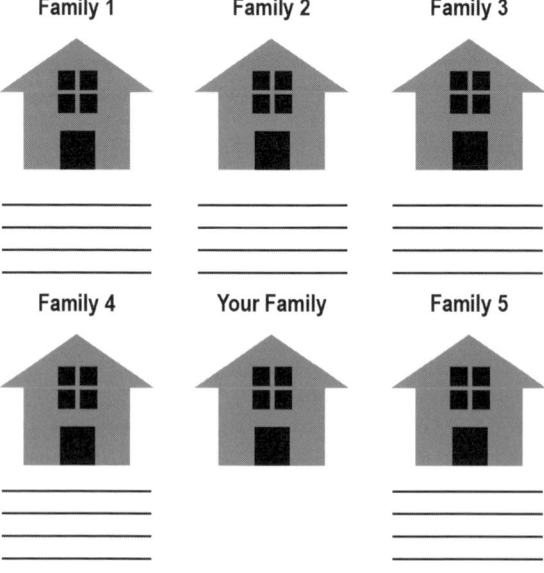

If you are like most of us, it is eye-opening how little we really know about our neighbors, and how little meaningful relationship actually exists. But what if things were different? What if we were to see the neighborhood in which we live as our primary mission field? (*Mission field* is a term used by evangelicals to define the territory of our response to the call to proclaim the Good News—even, as Francis of Assisi is oft quoted, "using words if necessary.")

As Kristin Schell puts it: "Too often the stumbling block to meeting our neighbors is the front door." [2]   Kristin is a mom, a wife, a lawyer, and a neighbor who realized that she wasn't being very neighborly. She felt called to develop relationships with her neighbors, so she responded by putting a turquoise picnic table in her front yard under a magnolia tree. Then she began to sit at that table every day, watching as her neighbors passed by taking their dogs for a walk, or couples strolled through the neighborhood, or moms rode bikes with their kids. At first she took her computer and some reading to keep her busy, not sure if anyone would actually stop to visit. But soon the table became a meeting place for people to come and hang out together. Neighbors became friends. Meaningful conversations began to happen. People began to care for one another. All because of a turquoise table.

Now, the turquoise table idea may not be the answer in your particular setting. But what would? How could you create space for neighbors to meet and gather and share and care?

There's even an app to help you get started. It's called Nextdoor, and it's a private social network designed to help neighbors stay in the know about what's going on in their own locale—from "finding a last-minute babysitter, learning about an upcoming block party, or hearing about a rash of car break-ins. There are many ways our neighbors can help us. We just need an easier way to connect with them." [3] Of course, that's just a technological tool that facilitates the process of connection. It's the connection itself—a result of thoughtful effort—that counts. Whether done by virtue of a modern day app or by as ancient and biblically authentic a method as walking next door in your sandals, having a way to communicate with neigh-

"JESUS IS MY EVERYTHING, A LOVING SAVIOR WHO LEADS AND LOVES ME EVERY DAY OF MY LIFE. HIS SHED BLOOD ON THE CROSS, HIS RESURRECTION AND PLAN OF SALVATION IS ALL THAT CAN SAVE US. ONLY JESUS HAS THAT POWER."

- FAYE, WEST DISTRICT, CTX CONF. UNITED METHODIST CHURCH

bors is really helpful. This was brought home to Phil by the recent experience of his father-in-law, who rented Phil's home for a year while Phil was away, and found himself a new face in an unfamiliar community. He is 91 years old, and while still self-sufficient, he has little interaction with people other than the waitresses who serve him most days at his favorite restaurant. His primary entertainment is watching the national cable news programs.

One afternoon, Phil's wife, Becky, saw on Facebook that a water main had broken in their old community, and all the residents were under a 'boil water' directive and had been for a couple of days. She called to make sure her dad knew about incident and found out he had absolutely no idea. There apparently had been no announcement about this local water main break on the national news show! It's a great example of the real-world difference that might be made if there were some form of communication network accessible to him and people like him within their own neighborhoods. Many of us live in areas where we could take leadership in establishing just such communication networks. It is a great way to care for and get to know other people and their needs.

Looking for such ways to be relevant and useful in our communities is in line with a ministry movement called *missional communities*, which bears out the kinds of things one would hope for in making our neighborhoods our mission field. The following definition is provided by the Soma Family of Churches:

> A **missional community** is a group of people, about the size of an extended family, who are united through Christian community around a common service and witness to a particular neighborhood or network of relationships. [4]

These communities grow out of an organic involvement in the life of the neighborhood. The goal is to become engaged in the lives of 20-40 persons in such a way that people connect the 'missionary' with the life of the community. Alan Hirsch, in *The Forgotten Ways Handbook*, suggests these simple modes of engagement:

- Living in the community.

- Spending time in local hang-out places.

- Walking your dog regularly.

- Doing your reading or work at a public location (library/ coffee shop).

- Joining community groups

- Developing a hobby that is useful for connecting with others. [5]

In many ways, this approach is similar to the outreach strategy practiced by the Celtic church (as developed by St. Patrick to bring Christianity to Ireland and beyond). St. Patrick came up with this new thinking as a refinement to the standard Roman Catholic evangelism approach that had been developed to convert the inhabitants of England:

> Bluntly stated, the Roman model for reaching people (who are civilized enough) is: (1) Present the Christian message; (2) Invite them to decide to believe in Christ and become Christians; and (3) If they decide positively, welcome them into the church and its fellowship. The Roman model seems very logical to us because most American evangelicals are scripted by it! We explain the gospel, they accept Christ, we welcome them into the church! Presentation, Decision, Assimilation.

> In contrast, this is the Celtic model for outreach: (1) You first establish community with people, or bring them into the fellowship of your community of faith; (2) Within the embrace of community, you engage in conversation, ministry, prayer and worship; (3) As people discover their gifts and faith, you invite them to commit to discipleship. [6]

Both the missional communities and Celtic outreach approaches start with a focus on building relationships, followed by ministry to those in the community, then followed by the invitation to discipleship. They are a living witness to the often quoted saying, "Christianity is more caught than taught."

There are two very strong factors at play in this approach:

First is the idea of **presence**. This is a term used by Alan Hirsch (a leader in the missional community movement) to describe the building of relationships. It is about being in empathetic connection to those persons in the same way that John describes the incarnation of Jesus:

> The Word became flesh and blood,
> and moved into the neighborhood.
> We saw the glory with our own eyes,
> the one-of-a-kind glory,
> like Father, like Son,
> Generous inside and out,
> true from start to finish. (John 14:14, *The Message*)

Phil likens the practice of presence to his experience in the neighborhood he moved into some 10 years ago. He got to know the neighbors to his left pretty quickly (Marty and Alina, a retired couple), since the gentleman was always out working in his yard. They would get together and have a drink out by the pool and keep each other caught up on what was happening with their spouses and kids. Ann, who lived directly across the street, was elderly, and they basically waved or had brief conversations as she was out getting her paper or mail—"How are you today? Hot isn't it?" That sort of thing. Betty Jo, who lived to their right, pretty much kept to herself, so the conversations with her, on the rare occasions when they couldn't help but cross paths, were even more basic. Then there was Billy, who lived a couple of doors down and walked his dog twice a day religiously (and by religiously, Phil doesn't mean it was a prayer walk—he means that Billy was dedicated and punctual in this activity). Billy and he regularly had conversations, but they never dipped much below the surface. These conversations were usually about the dogs or the weather or how the dogs were reacting to the weather.

See the pattern? Connections were being built, but there was no real involvement in each other's lives. They had no skin in the game.

Phil contrasts his ad-hoc, random neighborly interactions with the focused strategy of next-door-neighbor, Marty. Marty knew everybody in the neighborhood, and everybody in the neighborhood knew Marty. He was jovial and engaging and the kind of guy that just made people feel better by being around him. People would come from down the street and hang out in lawn chairs under Marty's carport. And if there was ever an opportunity for Marty to be involved in helping someone with a project, he was right there. Marty fixed leaky faucets, did landscaping, provided minor mechanical support when a car or an appliance wasn't working, and once he even wrangled a snake that had gotten into the house while Becky was home alone.

Alan Hirsch calls this **proximity**. It is about being involved in people's lives in ways that directly impact those people and witness to God's love for them. Hirsch describes it this way:

> This assumes not only presence but also genuine availability, which will involve spontaneity as well as regularity in the friendships and communities we inhabit. [7]

So, what would need to happen for us, the members of our congregations, and our churches to take the position of our neighborhoods being our mission fields?

First, the church needs to cast a vision for helping people discover the abundant life offered through a relationship with Jesus Christ. We should be regularly hearing about and discussing that concept in weekend worship messages, small groups discussions, and the vision casting of leadership teams. A series of questions posed by Adam Hamilton, senior pastor at the Church of the Resurrection, can guide such a conversation:

- Why Jesus? Does knowing Jesus have an impact in someone's life?

- Why church? Why is it important, or not? What can people get at church that they can't get anywhere else?

- Why this particular church? What's different about our church? Would I want to join this church if I weren't already a part of it?

If individual disciples and congregations filled with disciples can't answer these questions, it will be difficult to help others see the value in a relationship with Jesus or a connection to our particular community of faith.

Second, the church needs to recapture the expectation of being Great Commission disciples. This is our response to the directives given in the Great Commission, Jesus' post-resurrection parting instructions to the disciples before he ascended into Heaven.

> Therefore, go and make disciples of all nations, baptizing them in the name of the Father and of the Son and of the Holy Spirit, and teaching them to obey everything I have commanded you. (Matthew 28:19-20)

It is important (and consistent with our theme) to note that the word "go" is literally translated "as you go." Great Commission discipleship is not about handing out tracts or flyers, but adapting the routines of our daily lives (as we go) to the work of making disciples. The Great Commission is often used to support a focus on the valuable work of international missions, which takes its lead from the language of making disciples of all "nations." But what if that is too narrow a focus? "Nations," when translated literally, actually means "people groups." In truth, we are given valuable and accessible "people groups" right in our own neighborhoods.

Sometimes, as earnest and well-meaning disciples, we get hung up on the idea of "baptizing them." In our modern church structure, the performance of the sacrament of baptism is restricted to officially ordained clergy. This is an important acknowledgement of the sacred nature of the sacrament, and while we're not suggesting that we disregard the order of the church, maybe we should be careful not to get caught up in equating the sacrament of baptism with a decision to make a commitment to follow Jesus. Non-clergy people can be integral to helping others work through the process of deciding to enter into a relationship with Jesus Christ. In fact, that is part of our calling as disciples. It's not just professional ministry people who are supposed to be doing this critical work of welcoming new residents to God's kingdom: it's supposed to be all of us!

In order to recapture the imperative of the Great Commission in the everyday activities and neighborhoods in which disciples live (you and I, in our roles as regular folks doing our imperfect best to follow Christ), maybe it's a good time to revisit the core components of what it means to be a disciple of Jesus. What are the characteristics that define the lives of committed disciples? What are our priorities? In what activities are we engaged? What fruit do we produce?

One of the tools we have developed in our work to promote healthy congregations is a tool called the *Real Discipleship Survey*. It's an interactive Q&A that that invites disciples to describe their attitudes and actions in six dimensions of discipleship (a life of worship; a life of hospitality; a life of obedience; a life of generosity; a life of service; and a life of being open to Jesus). For each separate dimension, it helps individuals pinpoint how they are progressing on their journey from new faith to maturity. (It's available at our web site at www.emc3coaching.com, and you can take it is an individual or, even more powerfully, in conjunction with your entire congregation, in which case you get some eye-opening analytical reports about the strengths and weaknesses of your congregational family).

One of those dimensions is called **A Life of Hospitality**, and it is useful to help individuals and congregations identify how they're doing in offering the kind of hospitality that characterizes the lives of mature disciples. In the matrix included below, moving from left to right toward maturity, here are some of the measurable behaviors that distinguish how deeply we are modeling Christ's example of welcome and empathy:

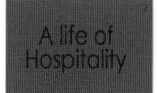

A life of Hospitality	I am curiously drawn to the Christians who graciously accept me as if I belong with them already.	I am called not only to receive, but also to offer God's gracious acceptance to others.	I seek to relate to others both in the church and beyond in ways that reflect God's hospitality to me.	I intentionally seek to build relationships with unchurched people in order to share God's love.

It's important to note that the foundational attitude which empowers the spirit of hospitality is acceptance. This begins with our own feeling of acceptance as we are welcomed into a community of believers, and increasingly, this deepening appreciation of our acceptance by the Creator informs our attitude and actions towards others. First, we learn the importance of accepting others within the body of Christ. As we grow, we move from simple acceptance to active engagement, demonstrating hospitality towards others in ways that naturally reflect the hospitality that has been shown to us. As we mature, we begin to intentionally build relationships with people outside the church to share God's love with them and to help them discover this love for themselves.

Based on the results of thousands of completed Real Discipleship Surveys (primarily in United Methodist congregations), the average percentage of disciples who place themselves in the maturing phase of development for a Life of Hospitality is somewhere around 5%. There are, of course, many factors at play here in explaining why more of us don't make it further in becoming more fully engaged in this ministry of welcome, but one of the most critical of these factors is that in our churches and small groups, we don't seem to teach, preach, or practice a focus on Incarnational Hospitality. We don't emphasize the intentional building of relationships so that those relationships may be an active expression of God's grace in someone else's life, providing a portal through which they may discover Christ's love for them.

Some congregations find it helpful to communicate this focus on Incarnational Hospitality as part of formal membership covenants. These statements of expectations use clear language to spell out our role as disciples within the local setting. Have you officially joined your local congregation? If so, can you recall your membership vows? Perhaps your church is one of those that actually offers members an opportunity to embrace a membership covenant (we are, after all, a covenant people). A written covenant clearly communicates the expectation of disciples to build up the body of believers and to be active witnesses to those beyond the church walls. An example of this kind of covenant is demonstrated below:

Traditional Vows	Dimensions of Discipleship	Membership Covenant
Prayers	Opening to Jesus/ Obeying Jesus	Participate regularly in a small discipleship group or other accountable discipling relationship.
Presence	A Life of Worship	Participate in weekly worship at least 3 weekends each month unless prevented by illness or travel.
Gifts	A Life of Generosity	Commit to proportional giving to the ministries of this congregation and to moving toward a tithe.
Service	A Life of Service	Serve in some way in the local community (beyond the walls of the church) each month.
Witness	A Life of Hospitality	Invite someone to come with me to church/events at least three times per year and build at least three relationships outside the church to witness the love of Christ.

You can see how participation in a covenant actually moves the discipleship conversation from the hypothetical to the concrete. One of the fundamental aspects of discipleship from the early church in Acts through the resurgence of the practical holiness of John Wesley's time was this commitment to accountability. Disciples walked with disciples, encouraging and nurturing one another, while also sharing an honest view of clearly stated goals for growth agreed to by the faith community. (For further discussion about membership covenants, you might find the resource, *Shift: Helping Congregations Back Into the Game of Effective Ministry*, helpful. [8])

Third, the church would need to make the building of relationships beyond the church itself a high priority. By this we mean that as disciples working together within the context of our local congregation, building relationships beyond our walls should be more important than getting people to our self-sponsored Bible studies, fellowship dinners, men's breakfasts, or even community service projects. That is not to say that there is anything wrong with these activities, only that our focus on them may be constricting our vision and depleting our resources in ways that may limit our options.

To gain insight into the possible impact of this potential shift in philosophy, Phil likes to employ an example from physics that stuck with him from his pre-pastoral career in Radiologic Sciences (x-ray technology). One of the basic principles in calculating x-ray intensities (or the intensity of lighting in photography) is called the Inverse Square Law. This law states that when you double the distance that an x-ray beam travels, the intensity of that x-ray beam loses three-quarters of its original intensity. The light at twice the distance has only one-fourth of the original intensity. When Phil shifted careers, a few years of ministry experience surprisingly revealed that this law turns out to also be a pretty good description of what happens to the intensity of the relationships a congregation has when one looks beyond the friendships they have established with their church-based Christian pals. Looking at the graph below, think about the horizontal axis as the number of years we have spent settling into our local church family and developing supportive relationships with our fellow disciples, and then look at how the vertical axis describes the number of deep community relationships we keep up with those outside of our congregational family activities. It many cases, the graph for committed, church-going disciples looks identical to the Inverse Square Law graphic on the next page.

Within a very short time of beginning our full-fledged participation in church activities, the number of non-church people we know and relate to in any meaningful way (our friends and acquaintances beyond our church family) drops precipitously. The more we engage in church-focused events that are held on church property, the more those external community relationships simply fade into the background.

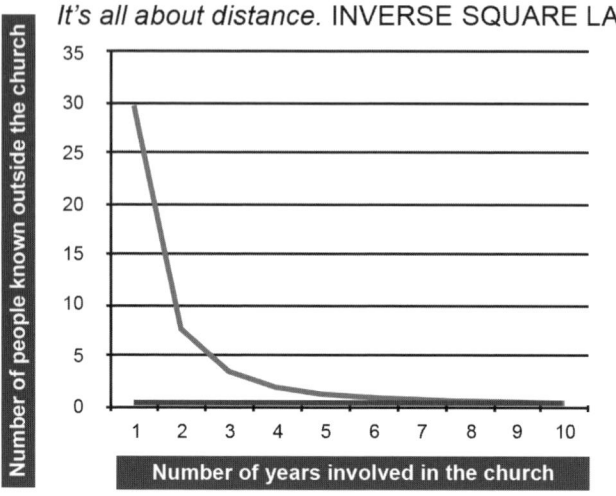

It's all about distance. INVERSE SQUARE LAW

As leaders in our churches and as boosters of our local congregations, we are guilty of unwittingly perpetuating this dilemma. What we should desire as we build a deeper understanding of discipleship within the support structure of our church is that everyone should be developing relationships outside the church—that's what our spiritual growth is equipping us for. We want followers of Christ to be the presence of Christ in the lives of people who don't yet know Christ, so that those people may come to know God's love for themselves. We want people in our congregations to invite others to come to church as an outgrowth of the caring connections we are already making in our communities, so that those people may discover for themselves how God offers new experiences for grace and growth within our congregations.

Yet . . .

Too often we have measured success in our local congregations by the participation levels in our church-sponsored activities and events at our physical church campus. We spend most of our time encouraging people to come to our fellowship dinners, our community service events, our prayer meetings, our fund raisers, our age-appropriate ministry gatherings, our gender-specific program groups, etc. We keep people so busy that they don't have time to be in relationships with those outside the church, and we celebrate when our church members get more and more active in church activities and events that perpetuate this circle of separating ourselves out of our old communities.

Then we turn around and wonder why it is so hard for people to invite their friends to worship or other special events. The answer is readily apparent: Many of us don't have any friends that don't already go to church.

What if we were instead at the forefront of a movement to change what our churches celebrated? (The old adage still applies that for people working in common purpose together, "You get what you celebrate.") So what if, instead, we helped lead our churches to new criteria for celebrations? What if we celebrated . . .

- Those that began to host neighborhood gatherings?

- Someone who started a book club in the neighborhood?

- Someone who brought a first-time guest to worship?

- Those who started a walking group in their community?

- A family that provided support for another family in their neighborhood during a time of crisis?

- Families who hosted block parties?

- Those who are leading prayer walks in their neighborhood?

You get the idea.

A **fourth key** is learning to be comfortable sharing our own personal faith stories. If you've missed opportunities to share your faith with others, even when an obvious opening to do so existed, it is likely that your local congregation hasn't given you a lot of focused help for carrying out this essential responsibility for all disciples. We talk a lot about sharing our witness, but it is rare that anybody walks us through exactly how to do that. We work with congregations of all sizes and in all geographic areas of the country to help them develop an intentional process of discipleship, but in the dozens and dozens of 'discipleship training' brochures/flyers we have reviewed in our coaching sessions, it is rare to see a single offering about how to build relationships with unconnected others or how to share our own personal faith story. Yet, this skill is one of the essential elements of Incarnational Hospitality. We're hopeful that the book you are holding right now will be a helpful guide for seeing yourself as a missionary in your own community, and that this current chapter might prompt you to encourage your own congregational leadership to do more to equip you and your fellow missionaries for loving, serving, and feeling confident about sharing your own story.

Sharing our faith story need not be difficult. Basically, it consists of developing our ability to articulate what life was like before we met Jesus, how we came to meet Jesus, and what life has been like since we first met Jesus (with an honest accounting of the struggles and triumphs along the way). The Apostle Paul gives a great example in Acts chapter 22:

Paul Before Christ

[Paul said] "Brothers and fathers, listen now to my defense."

When they heard him speak to them in Aramaic, they became very quiet. Then Paul said: "I am a Jew, born in Tarsus of Cilicia, but brought up in this city. I studied under Gamaliel and was thoroughly trained in the law of our ancestors. I was just as zealous for God as any of you are today. I persecuted the followers of this Way to their death, arresting both men and women and throwing them into prison, as the high priest and all the Council can themselves testify. I even obtained letters from them to their associates in Damascus, and went there to bring these people as prisoners to Jerusalem to be punished." (Acts 22:1-50)

Paul Receives Christ

"About noon as I came near Damascus, suddenly a bright light from heaven flashed around me. I fell to the ground and heard a voice say to me, 'Saul! Saul! Why do you persecute me?'

'Who are you, Lord?' I asked.

'I am Jesus of Nazareth, whom you are persecuting,' he replied. My companions saw the light, but they did not understand the voice of him who was speaking to me.

'What shall I do, Lord?' I asked.

'Get up,' the Lord said, 'and go into Damascus. There you will be told all that you have been assigned to do.' My companions led me by the hand into Damascus, because the brilliance of the light had blinded me.

A man named Ananias came to see me. He was a devout observer of the law and highly respected by all the Jews living there. He stood beside me and said, 'Brother Saul, receive your sight!' And at that very moment I was able to see him.

Then he said: 'The God of our ancestors has chosen you to know his will and to see the Righteous One and to hear words from his mouth. You will be his witness to all people of what you have seen and heard. And now what are you waiting for? Get up, be baptized and wash your sins away, calling on his name.'" (Acts 22:6-16)

Paul's Life with Christ

"When I returned to Jerusalem and was praying at the temple, I fell into a trance and saw the Lord speaking to me. 'Quick!' he said. 'Leave Jerusalem immediately, because the people here will not accept your testimony about me.'

'Lord,' I replied, 'these people know that I went from one synagogue to another to imprison and beat those who believe in you. And when the blood of your martyr, Stephen, was shed, I stood there giving my approval and guarding the clothes of those who were killing him.'

Then the Lord said to me, 'Go; I will send you far away to the Gentiles.'" (Acts 22:17-21)

Every disciple has a story to tell, and every disciple should be prepared to share their testimony, their story. Even those who received Christ at an early age have a story to tell (although they often don't feel as though they do). Some of them drifted away from that relationship and later found their way back. That is an important narrative as well. Some stayed constant, even as they struggled with doubt. That, too, is an important story.

Consider the 3-part outline below for sharing your personal journey in faith:

1. What was your life like before you entered into a relationship with Christ?

2. How did you come to know and be in a relationship with Christ?

3. How has this relationship with Christ made a difference in your life?

When we get to Chapter 6, we'll spend a significant amount of focused time developing our own personal stories. We'll flesh these ideas out in much greater detail.

In the meantime, here are some other resources that you may find helpful:

• *Contagious Christian*, Bill Hybels. [9]
• *Just Walk Across the Room*, Bill Hybels. [10]

- *The Forgotten Ways*, Alan Hirsch. [11]
- *Like Your Neighbor?*, Stephen Sorenson. [12]
- *Get Their Name*, Bob Farr, Doug Anderson, Kay Kotan. [13]

It is our hope that you will approach these ideas as not just another book study to provoke thought and conversation, but that you and your leadership teams will actually try out some of these suggestions and test their impact.

Thinking Outside the Box

The following approaches are highlighted as ways that disciples from our congregations can engage their neighbors in ways that will build relationships, minister to needs, and reflect the love of God:

Serve someone during a difficult time:

- Provide transportation to and from the doctor during a health crisis.
- Provide childcare when someone has to be away for some unexpected need.
- Provide meals for a family dealing with a hospitalization or loss.
- Share movies with someone who is recuperating.

Welcome newcomers to the neighborhood:

- Take a welcome gift—cookies, pie, or cake and some drinks.
- Offer to help unpack boxes.
- Invite them over for dinner, since the kitchen is not set up yet.
- Share insights into trusted mechanics, doctors, restaurants, etc.

Provide neighborhood gatherings:

- Have a cookout in your yard.
- Set up a play day for the kids.
- Host an outdoor movie night.
- Start a book club.

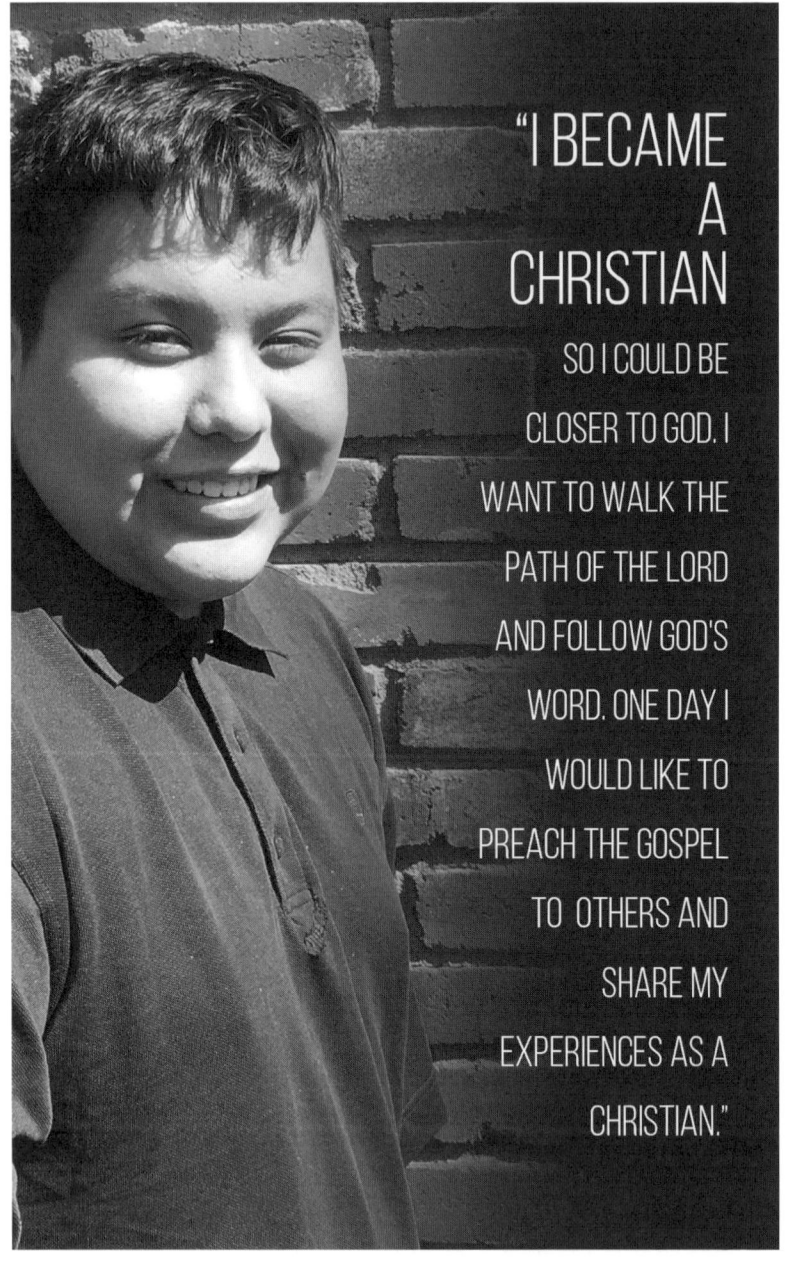

"I BECAME A CHRISTIAN SO I COULD BE CLOSER TO GOD. I WANT TO WALK THE PATH OF THE LORD AND FOLLOW GOD'S WORD. ONE DAY I WOULD LIKE TO PREACH THE GOSPEL TO OTHERS AND SHARE MY EXPERIENCES AS A CHRISTIAN."

- BENJAMIN, LINE STREET UNITED METHODIST CHURCH

- Invite neighbors over for a game night.
- Start a walking group.

Adopt a 'lonely person':

- Invite persons without local family connections for holiday gatherings.
- Have them over for a game night or movie night.

House watching services (ministries of security and safety):

- Offer to keep an eye on properties while neighbors are away.
- Establish a neighborhood watch.
- Collect mail while neighbors are away.
- Feed and walk dogs while neighbors are away.

Create a neighborhood map and contact list:

- Draw the neighborhood and identify the family for each home.
- Provide contact information for each home.

You can, of course, create a list several times this long. Think creatively and focus on things that uniquely match your specific skills and disposition as well as the skills and dispositions of others you might partner with in providing such hospitality—everything is more fun with a team. As you generate ideas, also be sure to include the needs of individual families receiving the hospitality, as well as the unique character of the community in which all of this is playing out.

For example, the good people of First Brownwood United Methodist Church in Brownwood, Texas (just east of Dallas), looked around their town and noticed that the local institution of higher learning, Howard Payne University, had an official "move in" day for the young adults returning for fall semester. They decided to take a big group of strong, friendly folks from their church and show up to help. They spent the day carrying suitcases and boxes to dorm rooms and helping arrange furniture. Then they brought the kids back to the church that night for a really nice dinner. (And although Howard Payne is a Baptist University, there sure do seem to be a lot of college kids at Brownwood UMC!)

Relationships matter.

Supporting Relational Development

In addition to the factors discussed previously, there are lots of other ways that you can join forces with your fellow disciples and encourage an institutional focus on developing community relationships:

- **Neighborhood Gatherings**: Instead of doing a cookout on the grounds of the church, the equipment and supplies—and maybe even a cooking team—could be provided to support neighborhood events.

- **Backyard Bible Clubs**: Instead of having everyone come to the church for a children's ministry gathering, recruit families in neighborhoods around the community to provide these. Train these families and provide the resources they need to be successful. Imagine the possibilities of reaching children who may never make it to an activity located on the church property.

- **Barnyard Bible Clubs** (for you congregations where barns are more prevalent than subdivision walls): Morgan Mills UMC had a strong ladies' Bible Study which met at the church, but the men just wouldn't come. The pastor asked to use the barn of a local homestead and invited everybody to a Bible Study on location there. It turned out to be one of the best attended Bible Studies ever in that county.

- **Vacation Bible School** in the Community: Several churches we are working with have moved VBS from a week-long event at the church to a one-day event offered in parks/recreational areas in neighborhoods around the community.

They are engaging lots of children who would not typically participate in a church focused event.

- **Block Parties**: Encourage families to host block parties once or twice a year. Provide them with resources like bouncy houses and big grills.

Jesus actually means for us to love our neighbors—those right around us in our neighborhoods, as well as those we meet on the roads of life. Such love is not an abstract concept. It implies relationship.

Eddie recently heard the story of a Midwest congregation that took its responsibility to support neighborhood gatherings seriously. They bought a trailer and stocked it with a 'party to go' set up. There was a big grill for cooking bunches of hotdogs and hamburgers at the same time. A couple of different bouncy houses were provided for entertaining the kids. A stack of lawn chairs was included. It was even stocked with paper goods and utensils. It had everything that was needed to host a gathering, along with all the instructions about how to set it all up and pack it all back in the trailer again afterwards. And anybody could use this trailer for free, just by reserving it for a day. They would even tow it to your neighborhood if you didn't have a truck and a trailer hitch.

That's institutional support for loving your neighbors! The congregations that seem to be the most successful at helping participants engage those in the community are the ones that are most intentional about emphasizing the importance of this goal, while providing the support to make it happen.

A pastor friend of Phil's named Jack Stephenson served one of the faster growing congregations in the Florida Conference of the United Methodist Church. There were many reasons for the vitality of this congregation, but one was that they were intentional about connecting with their neighbors. The community surrounding his church was divided up into smaller mission fields, with a mission leader for each designated area responsible for getting people connected and welcoming newcomers to the neighborhood. Each leader was provided with new mover information for his or her area, and each made it a priority to have newcomers to the neighborhood greeted by a church member who lived in the same neighborhood. If needs arose in the community (fire in the home, loss of loved one, medical crisis), the team leader had access to resources to support the family in need.

It could be said that this is just the church being the church—that is, the people who make up the church being good neighbors. Just like Jesus said.

Questions and Exercises for Individuals

1. When you read Luke 10:25-37 (the story of the Good
   Samaritan), what do you take away regarding Jesus' meaning as to
   who our neighbors are? What interpretations of this passage have
   you been exposed to over the years? Did this chapter's discussion
   of the passage change or expand your thinking in any way?

2. Can you see yourself doing something like the turquoise table in
   your neighborhood (or maybe you already are)? What are some
   ways you could boost your neighborly interactions?

3. In what ways is the church you currently attend a missional
   church, as discussed in this chapter? In what ways is it definitely
   not a missional church (internally-focused rather than interested
   in the community beyond its walls)? What would be the biggest
   opportunities to be more missional and what would be the
   biggest obstacles?

4. Could you give coherent answers for the questions posed on
   page 53 if they came up in conversation with someone you had
   recently met: Why Jesus? Why church? And why this particular
   church?

5. Where would you place yourself on the hospitality continuum laid out on page 55? How could you be more focused on offering hospitality?

6. If you were in charge of designing a Membership Covenant for a local church, what specific things would it include?

7. This chapter included the aphorism, "you get what you measure," which states that we generally get results based on the specific criteria by which we measure success. How does your congregation measure success—what things get counted? How do you measure your own success as a disciple? What are your personal benchmarks for growth?

8. Given the opportunity, are you prepared to share your personal faith story? What parts of your own story do you sense are the most interesting to other people? What parts make you uncomfortable or self-conscious?

9. Did the examples on pages 63-65 of ways to love and serve others make you think of particular people? Go back through and jot down some possibilities.

Discussion and Activities for Small Group Settings

In addition to comparing your individual responses to the questions from the preceding pages, as well as the group activities suggested within the chapter, give some thoughts to the more institutionally oriented questions below.

1. How could the congregation of which you are a part cast a vision for helping people discover an abundant life with Jesus?

2. How could your church communicate clear expectations for individual disciples to build relationships and share their faith?

3. What things could your church celebrate that would help move your congregation from an internal focus to an external focus?

4. What are some ways your congregation could begin to train people in faith sharing?

5. How could your church encourage and support the development of relationships in the neighborhoods around it?

• CHAPTER 3 •
CIRCLE OF INFLUENCE

About 25 years ago, Phil and Becky discovered a Tex-Mex restaurant in Fort Lauderdale, while attending a convention just down the road. It looked like a hole-in-the-wall kind of place from the outside (which, of course, appeals to Phil anyway), but it turned out to be a larger and more popular establishment than it looked. It also turned out to have some of the best Tex-Mex food that they had eaten anywhere, and Phil travels a lot!

The salsa was incredibly fresh, and they made hand-pressed corn tortillas which, with a little butter, made the perfect appetizer. The Tacos al Carbon were amazing. And to top it off was their version of 'fried ice cream,' which wasn't actually fried but had that same crunchy texture, with chocolate, caramel, and homemade whipped cream topping.

It was such a memorable experience that they make it a point to stop by whenever they are in the area, and sometimes they'll even make the drive if they're within a couple of hours travel time. The experience was too good to keep to themselves, so they began to tell their extended family and friends, and even to take some of them along occasionally. Over the years, Phil estimates that somewhere between 40-50 lucky people have visited that restaurant based on their recommendation.

Eddie has a mechanic he feels that same way about. His name is Byron, and his shop is called Byron's, and it doesn't have a fancy sign out front. Byron and his assistant, Mike, wear worn-out jeans, not a crisp uniform. But what they do is work magic with old, beat up cars (the kind that Eddie prefers to drive). They say things like, "Aw, you can drive another 10,000 miles before you need to get that wheel bearing fixed. Just bring it back in when the noise gets where you can't stand it anymore." Eddie was introduced to Byron years ago by his good friend, Gary. And likewise, Eddie has passed along this sacred knowledge of the cheap and dependable mechanic to dozens of now-loyal customers.

We've all had those kinds of experiences. For all of us, sharing something that we have really enjoyed or have found beneficial just seems to come naturally. When we read a good book, we are very likely to tell a friend whom we think might enjoy it. When we see a good movie, we tell our friends. When we find a great place to eat or cool activity or interesting exhibit or a great new song, we become walking, talking infomercials for anybody who will listen. It just seems natural to pass the word along or invite our friends to make the same discovery.

The same thing should apply to our experience with Jesus. It hopefully even applies to the place where we have built a community that grows closer to Jesus together: our local church homes, the ones in which we are part of unique, Jesus-centered communities. When we have discovered something special, it is just natural to share.

This is not a new phenomenon. In fact, we even see it demonstrated in the Scriptures. One excellent example is found early in the gospel of John:

> The next day Jesus decided to leave for Galilee. Finding Philip, he said to him, "Follow me." Philip, like Andrew and Peter, was from the town of Bethsaida. Philip found Nathanael and told him, "We have found the one Moses wrote about in the Law, and about whom the prophets also wrote—Jesus of Nazareth, the son of Joseph."

> "Nazareth! Can anything good come from there?" Nathanael asked. "Come and see," said Philip. When Jesus saw Nathanael approaching, he said of him, "Here truly is an Israelite in whom there is no deceit." "How do you know me?" Nathanael asked. Jesus answered, "I saw you while you were still under the fig

tree before Philip called you." Then Nathanael declared, "Rabbi, you are the Son of God; you are the king of Israel." Jesus said, "You believe because I told you I saw you under the fig tree. You will see greater things than that." He then added, "Very truly I tell you, you will see 'heaven open, and the angels of God ascending and descending on' the Son of Man." (John 1:43-59)

There are several kernels of wisdom to be gleaned from this scripture passage. First, there seem to be a variety of ways that people are invited into a relationship with Jesus. Sometimes it is a direct invitation ("Finding Philip, he said, 'Follow me.'") Other times it is through someone who has already discovered Jesus as the Messiah (the one who has come to save). Statistically, somewhere between 60-80% of people who get involved with a local church and discover Jesus do so because of the invitation of a friend who has already made that discovery for themselves.

As powerful as this personal, enthusiastic invitation can be, it is a curious fact that we can be uniquely shy about sharing our faith or talking about the church where we worship. We'll shout to the high heavens about the new *Star Wars* movie, *Game of Thrones* episode, or the latest burger bistro, but we are hesitant to talk about the work of Jesus in our own lives. Some of this is a sensitivity to not offending others in a politically correct world; some of it is a fear of rejection of something very important to us; some of us is just a realization as to how skeptical people can be concerning spiritual values and the communities of people who embrace them.

Of course, even way back in the Gospel accounts, people often responded to Jesus' invitation with skepticism: "Can anything good come from Nazareth?" This is certainly no less true for the church today. People routinely ask, "Can anything good come from the church?" It doesn't advance our cause to become defensive about this state of affairs, dismissive of this skepticism, or reticent to share because of it. Our most helpful approach would be to try to understand it better and perhaps respond to it with empathy. The perspective of those who are skeptical of our enthusiasm for the church was highlighted a few years ago in a research study called the Fermi Project. Consider the following statistics: [1]

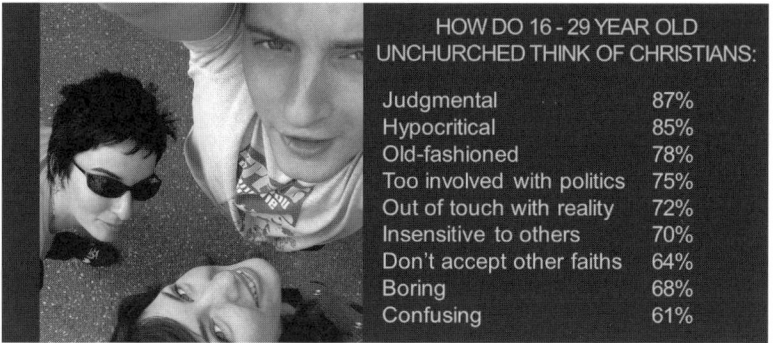

HOW DO 16 - 29 YEAR OLD UNCHURCHED THINK OF CHRISTIANS:	
Judgmental	87%
Hypocritical	85%
Old-fashioned	78%
Too involved with politics	75%
Out of touch with reality	72%
Insensitive to others	70%
Don't accept other faiths	64%
Boring	68%
Confusing	61%

As you read that chart, some of you were already thinking, "Yeah, but these are 16-29 year olds. They don't like anything!" Of course, historically, many of us were once in the category of young people who turned away from the organized church only to come back home when we decided to settle down and start families, but for numerous denominations this is the first time they are experiencing a phenomenon in which those young people just aren't ever returning. Every church we are working with is trying to figure out how to get more (or any!) of this age group into their doors. It would probably be wise to recognize the issues they have with the church and assess to what degree they are right about us. We should also point out that these perspectives are not limited to this age group. With more than half of the people in any given geographic area not connected to any type of faith community, it is clear that the world around us doesn't seem to have a value-added perspective about the impact and relevance of the church.

So, if people don't seem to think much of the church, why would they even bother coming? This brings us to the third insight from this text.

Nathanael came because he trusted Philip. He came because of their friendship.

And it is certainly worth noting that **Nathanael may have come initially because he trusted Philip, but he stayed because he discovered Jesus**: "Rabbi, you are the Son of God; you are the king of Israel."

People still come to Jesus because friends invite them.

It seems like such a simple statement. But it is full of implications. We live in a world where the word "friend" has taken on a whole new meaning. Consider the following quote from Kit Yarrow's *Decoding the New Consumer Mind*:

> We live in a society that is, in some senses, more connected than ever. We can easily develop relationships with fellow dog lovers and wine lovers, and even with future lovers we've yet to meet in person. We can stay in touch with classmates and colleagues whom we no longer see in person. We can share our opinions with strangers we'll never meet. It's a paradox of our era that, although we have more "friends" than ever, we increasingly feel unheard, unseen, disconnected or alone. At the very least, it calls into question the quality of these many connections. [2]

The quality of friendship we are talking about here is different from having hundreds of "friends" on Facebook. While those friends may have a multitude of connections (mutual friends/people you may know), the vast majority, in most people's experience, are really just connections. The quote captures the difference between real friendship and faux friendship: real friends don't leave us unheard, unseen, disconnected, or alone.

Which means that there is a strong relational component out of which trust is built, as illustrated by this acrostic:

T **Truth**: Willingness to speak truth into someone's life.

R **Reliability**: Being there for someone in good times and bad.

U **Understanding**: Connected at a level that promotes understanding of how the person thinks and the joys and concerns playing out in that person's life.

S **Support**: Willingness to offer ourselves and our resources to meet someone's needs.

T **Time/Togetherness**: Relationships that grow out of time spent in development.

All of this is, of course, fueled by the witness of our own lives. If our relationship with Christ is not making a difference in the way we live, the ways we interact with others, the decisions we make, the ways we use our resources, the ways we set our priorities, and the ways we serve, it will be difficult for anyone to see why they should seek out that kind of relationship for themselves.

Finally, there is the issue of being able to communicate with our friends the difference Jesus is making in our own lives. Ours is a results-oriented society, and since authentic discipleship definitely comes with a cost, it's not unreasonable to be prepared to offer up a cost-benefit analysis of our lives devoted to Christ. As noted previously, the Apostle Peter reminds us:

> Always be prepared to give an answer to everyone who asks you to give the reason for the hope you have. (1 Peter 3:15)

Of course, our investment in discipleship scores emphatically on the benefits side. We should be thoughtful and enthusiastic about communicating that. If you have not thought through (prepared) a framework for presenting your own personal faith story, consider using the process we share in the final chapter of this book.

"TO ME, JESUS IS MY LORD AND SAVIOR. WHILE THAT IS TRUE, IT SOUNDS "CHURCHY" AND WITNESSING TO OTHERS SHOULDN'T COME OFF THAT WAY. AND SO, I WOULD SAY HE IS MY BEST FRIEND AND CONFIDANT AND THE ONE I TRUST WITH MY LIFE.."

- RUTH, LINE STREET UNITED METHODIST CHURCH

All of this philosophical underpinning leads us to the idea of actually issuing an invitation to a real, flesh-and-blood human being. Statistically, it is depressing to note the astonishing fact that in United Methodist circles (Phil and Eddie's mainstream denominational tribe), the average churchgoer invites someone to come to worship with them about once every 38 years! Bob Farr, Kay Kotan, and Doug Anderson have put into writing what we've been teaching for years about making such an invitation:

> Why do mainline church members so very infrequently invite others to worship? One reason is that we often mistake a wish for an invitation. We tell someone, "I'd like for you to come to worship some time at my church." But this is not an invitation—it is simply a wish, with little chance of being fulfilled. **An invitation has three characteristics:**
>
> 1. It is **personal** (phone to phone, face to face or Facebook to Facebook).
>
> 2. It is **specific** ("I want to invite you to come on May 13 at 10 o'clock for worship and lunch afterward.").
>
> 3. It is **relational** ("I want to invite you to come with me to worship on May 13th. Would you like for me to pick you up?"). [3]

It goes without saying that the probability of a positive response is pretty much 100% greater if this is someone with whom you have a pre-existing relationship. Just walking up to someone on the street and inviting to come along with you to worship is not the best bet for success. It takes a little time to build some credibility as an instrument of God's grace. As Alan Hirsch puts it in *The Forgotten Ways Handbook*:

> When we hang out as representatives of Jesus, people get the idea that God is interested in fostering a relationship with them. [4]

Jim Ozier, in his book *Clip-In*, suggests that it might be helpful to work people toward issuing such invitations by helping them learn how to recommend their church. He feels this would be a big step forward for most disciples and churches. The following graphic shows the flow toward inviting developed by Ozier: [5]

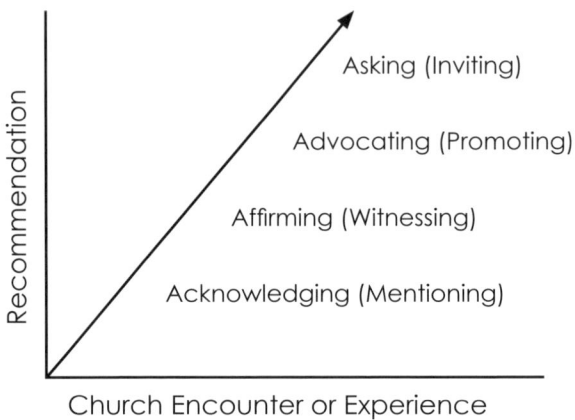

Asking (Inviting)

Advocating (Promoting)

Affirming (Witnessing)

Acknowledging (Mentioning)

Recommendation

Church Encounter or Experience

Getting Started

So how do we begin to consider with whom to build the kind of relationships that matter (connections established by us that provide people a natural pathway to the discovery that Jesus offers a life-changing relationship to them)? One way to begin is to look at your circle of influence. Using the following diagram:

• Within the inner circle, place smaller circles with initials identifying persons who have influenced your journey in faith.

• In the second circle out, identify family members and close friends with whom you could share life more fully, thus creating opportunities to more fully share your faith story.

• In the third circle out, identify co-workers, acquaintances, neighbors, or people you engage in conversation while your kids are on the ball field. These are people for whom you will pray and seek opportunities to engage more deeply in relationship, share your story, and invite them to discover a relationship with Jesus.

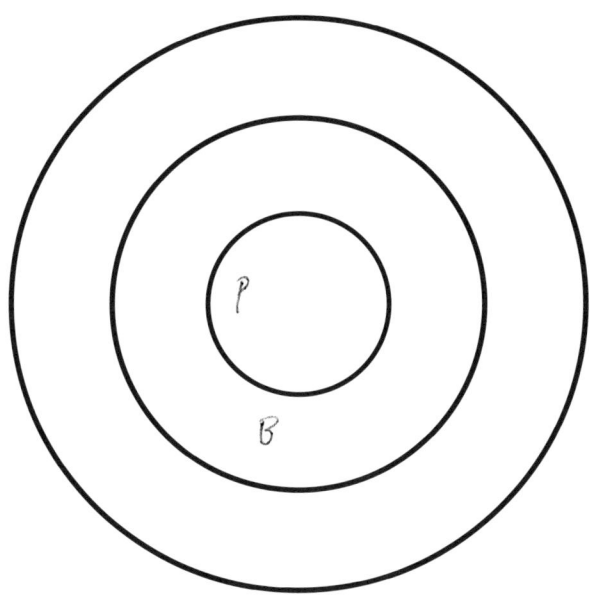

In a very strong sense, we are inviting you to see those in your circle of influence as your personal mission field. They are the ones with whom God has placed you in relationship so that you might be the conduit for their discovery of God's love for them.

There are several useful keys to engaging those in your mission field (circle of influence). A couple of these were introduced in the previous chapter, but they are definitely worth reviewing, because they are critical to helping us rethink the possibilities of how we interact with the people who are already a part of our day.

You'll remember that the missional church movement leader Alan Hirsch focused on a familiar passage straight out of the Gospel to capture the idea of presence. It is a term used to describe our accessibility and openness to relationships. It is about being intentionally available to the people we encounter in the same way that Jesus made himself available (as described by the Apostle John):

The Word became flesh and blood,
and moved into the neighborhood.
We saw the glory with our own eyes,
the one-of-a-kind glory,
like Father, like Son,
generous inside and out,
true from start to finish. (John 1:14, *The Message*)

We've seen that passage before, but reading those words again, spend a few moments to think about whether people see you as a reflection of God's grace—do you bring God's identifiable glory to your neighborhood, workplace, or school? Hirsch explains the link between presence and the greater mission:

[T]he idea of presence highlights the role of relationships in mission. If relationship is the key means in the transfer of the gospel, then it simply means we are going to have to be directly present to the people in our circle. Our very lives are our messages, and we cannot take ourselves out of the equation of mission. But one of the profound implications of our presence as representatives of Jesus is that Jesus actually likes to hang out with the people we hang out with. They get the implied message that God actually likes them. [6]

The second part of this relationship engagement, as we explored in the previous chapter, is what Hirsch refers to as **proximity**. It is about being involved in people's lives in ways that impact those lives and witness to God's love and concern for them:

Jesus mixes with people from every level of society. He ate with Pharisees as well as tax collectors and prostitutes. If we are to follow in his footsteps, his people will need to be directly and actively involved in the lives of the people we are seeking to reach. This assumes not only presence but genuine availability, which will involve spontaneity as well as regularity in the friendships and communities we inhabit. [7]

A third key to practicing Incarnational Hospitality in our circle of influence is **authenticity**. Authenticity is a sense on behalf of the people that encounter us that we are sincere about living out what we believe. It is an honesty that allows us to be less than perfect, and to admit that we are broken. We're not just putting on some kind of religious act. We are engaging hard questions in honest conversation with God and our fellow believers.

Most everybody is frustrated with inauthenticity. You know the drill. The phone rings and the person calling starts the conversation by stating that "this is not a sales call." Then they go on to ask a bunch of questions about you that you may or may not feel comfortable answering. Then they try to 'sell' you something to meet some predetermined need they think you have and that the questions are designed to bring to the surface.

You can smell them a mile away! Usually you hang up before the questions even get started, making some kind of excuse like "I'm just walking out the door and don't have time to talk right now." There's nothing authentic about them. The same smell test applies to Christians who are looking to get another "notch in their belt" by building a relationship just to get someone to come to church.

Incarnational Hospitality is lived out in *authentic* relationships. These are characterized by:

- **Acceptance**: How do you relate to and welcome those
  who are different from you? In nature, "birds of a feather
  flock together." But in the Kingdom of God, everyone is
  welcomed. This was hard for the early church to hear. The
  Holy Spirit expanded the early church's understanding
  of the inclusiveness of the Kingdom story by story, as if a
  bulldozer were knocking down every cultural barrier that
  kept people apart. Could sinners be welcomed? Could tax
  collectors and prostitutes? Could Greek-speaking Jews?
  Could Gentile God-fearers? Could Roman soldiers? Could

godless Gentiles? Could those who had been worshiping foreign gods? The answer repeatedly was, "Yes!" God's welcome includes even them. And the early church struggled to welcome all of these different people into their table fellowship. How about you and your church? Who might not feel welcomed if they showed up at your small group or if they found themselves kneeling beside you during communion? Jesus seemed to purposefully hang out with people who were not like him. What's more, these outsiders seemed to be drawn to his company. When you hang out with people not like you, are they drawn to you?

- **Forgiveness**: Jesus said, "Blessed are the peacemakers" (Matthew 5:9). Paul said, "If it is possible, as far as it depends on you, live at peace with everyone" (Romans 12:18). How do you relate to people with whom you do not agree or who have hurt you? Jesus said that even sinners are nice to those who like and affirm them. "Love your enemies" (Matthew 5:44). "Bless those who curse you, pray for those who mistreat you" (Luke 6:28). Make peace with those who have hurt you. Our culture is strong on individual rights, on stressing what WE deserve, and on what WE are entitled to in relationships. Jesus turned much of this upside down and said to those for whom he died while we were yet sinners, "Love each other as I have loved you." (John 15:12)

- **Accountability**: The Apostle Paul scatters throughout his letters the 'one anothers' that provide insight into how we are to do life together. A central theme in these 'one anothers' is that of accountability, expressed in a variety of ways: Submit to one another, encourage one another, admonish one another, bear with one another, agree with one another, and live in harmony with one another. Authentic relationships include accountability.

A fourth key to engaging those in your mission field (circle of influence) is **compassion**. This word comes from the Latin "com" (with) + "pati" (to suffer, to bear—and in this case, to bear also means to carry, as in carrying one another's burden). It is about engaging in the suffering or misfortune of another, often including the desire to alleviate it. When we have compassion for someone, we don't just feel sorry for them. We engage them in some way. We become involved in their lives in a way that brings help and hope.

A fifth key to engaging your personal mission field is that of developing **an awareness of "thin places."** In the Celtic tradition, thin places are physical settings that provide an opening into the wonder and majesty of God. Sharlande Sledge describes it this way (beautifully, we might add):

"Thin places," the Celts call this space,
Both seen and unseen,
Where the door between the world
And the next is cracked open for a moment
And the light is not all on the other side.
God shaped space. Holy. [8]

There are also some "thin places" that are less physical spaces and more emotional or life event focused. These are places where people seem to be more open to the ministry of God's people and the working of God's Spirit in their lives. Consider the following suggestions. You will have no trouble thinking of more based on your life experiences.

- **Marriage:** It is not uncommon for people to choose to be married in a church setting or at least by a pastor, even if they are not practicing Christians. Deep down there is a sense that this act is more than a legal transaction. There is a spiritual dimension. This of course opens the opportunity to have spiritual conversations.

- **Birth of a child**: Parents want the best for their children. They want to give them every benefit. Even for those not active in a community of faith, there is often a request for the child to be baptized or an opening for a friend to engage in conversation about this opportunity. This can lead to other spiritual conversations.

• **Moving Day**: The transition into a new community is a time of much uncertainty. We have left friends and support networks behind, and are not sure how to reestablish these essential life components. An invitation to participate in a faith community brings the potential for instant relationships and support. Many people, even if not regularly involved previously, may be open to this invitation.

• **Loss of a Loved One**: The death of a family member or close friend is a time at which a person is both confronted with their own mortality and sensing a great loss in their world as they have known it. The support offered during this time, whether formal (e.g. providing funeral services) or personal (e.g. just being there as a friend) can lead to significant faith conversations.

• **Divorce**: Much like the loss of loved one through death, divorce brings a great sense of disorientation and sometimes even failure or guilt. The support offered during this time, whether formal (e.g. grief support groups) or personal (e.g. just being there as a friend), can open the door to significant faith conversations.

• **Aging**: In a culture that seems to place youth on a pedestal, there is sometimes a profound sense of grief, disengagement, loneliness, and loss of self-worth. The support offered during this time of life can be transformative.

• **Loss of a Job**: Whether through downsizing or forced early retirement or simply things not working out, the loss of a job is a traumatic experience. It is an opportunity to offer support formally (e.g. resume development, job training) or personally (e.g. just being there as a friend).

• **Health Concerns**: Whether struggling through chemotherapy for cancer, wrestling with an addiction, or suffering with a severe illness or injury, it is the rare person who does not want someone to be there for them and to pray for them.

There is a stress test called the Life Change Index Scale, available in several forms online (e.g. the Holmes-Rahe Stress inventory)—we suggest taking it yourself as an informative exercise. [9] Diagnostic tools such as this reinforce the reality that any of these life changing events (and any number of others not listed here) actually affect us beyond just our state of mind; they also can impact our physical heath. Access to a wider community to help carry the load is welcomed by most people facing stressful times. Let's be unequivocally clear: we're not suggesting that all disciples should be trained as mental health counselors (or even act as amateur counselors, as well-intentioned Christians are sometimes prone to do). We're suggesting, however, that all disciples should develop an awareness of these "thin places" which are an everyday part of people's lives, so that they are prepared to respond to opportunities to offer themselves in relationship, witness to the presence of God, and even share stories about how God has been at work in their own lives.

Such vulnerability and accessibility often lead to deeper conversations, particularly when dealing with the existential questions commonly triggered by time spent in the "thin places" of difficult change. And just as we can be ready to give an accounting of our faith (our personal testimony) and our witness to how God has been at work in and through us, we can also be prepared to help someone else—should the occasion arise—to take steps toward entering a relationship with Jesus as their own Lord and Savior. The following framework may be a helpful tool:

God's grace for all.

Recognizing and repenting of sin.

Accepting God's forgiveness.

Confessing faith in Jesus Christ.

Engaging life as a disciple of Jesus.

A sample of this framework with expanded themes and Scriptures for reflection is found in the appendices of this book.

While the idea of a 'formula' may be intimidating, this invitation to someone to begin a relationship as a disciple of Jesus is actually a fairly natural conversation. Phil relates his own experience way back in the day when, as a volunteer youth director, he had this conversation with a guy called Ray. Ray came from a fairly rough background and had become involved in the youth ministry primarily because he could play the drums in the worship band. After months of participation and several superficial level conversations, they finally had an opportunity to really talk about his relationship with Jesus. It began with the question, "Does Jesus really forgive everything like you've been saying?" They talked about grace and it being freely given—not earned. Ray shared some of the things that he wasn't sure could be forgiven, and when Phil reassured him that, yes, God forgives even those things, Ray accepted that forgiveness for himself. Then they prayed together, with Ray asking Jesus into his life. Phil can't remember whether they used some 'official' prayer, but it was a powerful time nonetheless. Over the next couple of years, Ray became a leader in the youth ministry and continued to grow in his relationship with Christ.

In a very similar way, but a completely different context many years later, Phil had the opportunity to share in conversation with a highly successful business executive. They were in a general conversation about values and priorities, when the dialogue pivoted to Jesus as a specific priority (indeed, *the* specific priority). This executive, Bill, had been going to church for a while, but mostly because his wife wanted him to go, and he also thought it probably didn't hurt his image from a PR standpoint for others to see him participating. Bill acknowledged that, in truth, Jesus was actually a pretty low priority for him. But then, as a result of an introspective and honest conversation—and Phil primarily functioning as a good listener— Bill made a commitment to change things. His approach to life and commitment hadn't really been working so well anyway. He made a confession of faith in Jesus—an "I will follow you all the way" kind of confession—and they prayed together. In the years that followed, they had many lively conversations about Bill's adventures as a growing disciple of Jesus.

These conversations aren't rocket science. They don't require a seminary degree or an orator's certificate. It's a matter of keeping it simple and keeping it real.

It is important that we remember that our call is not to get people on their knees to pray (although that is sometimes the natural outcome of such honesty and vulnerability). Just as we are called to always be growing our own relationship with Jesus, we are also called to help others grow in their own relationships with God, and that process starts from wherever they happen to be on the journey when we first encounter them (and wherever we happen to be on our journey when they encounter us—maybe just a little farther down the path). We can't force that process. We can't push them ahead to GO and "collect our $200 spiritual reward." We meet them where they are, forging an authentic, relevant relationship that prepares the ground for what comes next.

Phil's friend, Kim, shares a story which is a reminder about this link to a deeper relationship with Christ:

> Several years ago, while my husband and I were planting a new church, a young African American woman came to our door selling magazines. She was happy to have water and a snack while she talked to us about the magazines she was selling. Evidently, she was working with a company that dropped magazine sellers into a neighborhood in the morning and picked them up much later in the day. We enjoyed talking with her around the kitchen table as we looked through her magazine information.
>
> Now, as church planters, we were enthusiastic about sharing our faith stories anyway, but the opportunity came because this young woman asked questions about the kinds of magazines we were choosing. In the course of the conversation we led her to Christ, prayed with her, gave her a Bible, and then sent

her on her way.

After she walked to the next door, I looked at my husband and said "What have we done? She is not connected to anyone! How will she grow in her new faith?" My heart has grieved this experience for years! Not because we led her to Jesus, but because we did not have a relationship with her! We could not be her friends who could journey with her through life. I don't remember her name or her face, but whenever this experience comes to mind, I pray for this young woman! My prayer has always been: "Provide people for her who will love her and help her to know Jesus more fully. Help her to find purpose and meaning through her relationship with Jesus."

While the primary way that people are invited into a relationship with Jesus is through personal relationships and faith sharing (incarnational hospitality), there are significant ways that your church can support the process.

Another of Phil's pastor friends tells this story that relates just how effectively an organized and focused ministry can build and support relationships:

I once went to a Billy Graham crusade in Arkansas and wanted to see what would happen if I walked down onto the field. Within one minute I was met by a woman of similar age who talked and prayed with me and handed me the Book of John and some other devotional materials. Then she called me and stayed connected with me for the next three months. Also, the next day my name was given to the Methodist church in town and they connected with me in every way possible. I learned that the Graham people spent six months before every campaign teaching people from every kind of church how to lead and partner new people of faith. Not only that, but the Graham people also stayed six months *after* every campaign to be sure every person was fully connected to a church. Follow-up matters.

Of course, not every religious organization has the prodigious resources of "the Graham people," but every fellowship of believers can find the strategies that work for them. The following are a few of the things we have used over the years. You will certainly have no trouble brainstorming more (including a few that are unique to your specific community), and if your church isn't already making these kinds of resources available, you can be a catalyst for making them new tools for connectional ministry.

- **Business Cards for Members**: it is always easier to invite someone to church if you have something to give them that provides basic information. The simplest form of this is a business card. As you can see from the sample below it includes a place for the member to write in their name and phone number, and on the back it includes a map providing directions to the church and the established worship times.

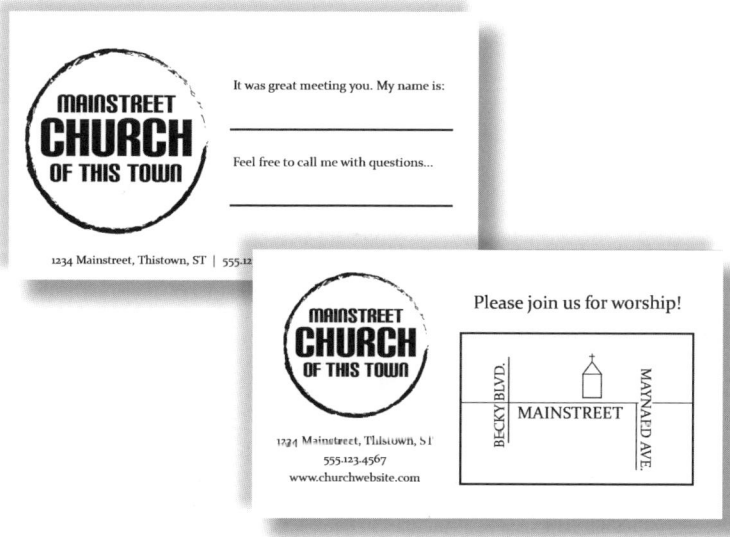

- **Seasonal/Series Flyers or Postcards**: It is common practice in many congregations to provide some form of marketing tool that participants in worship can take with them to share with family, friends, neighbors, and co-workers. This can be done at the start of a new message series or the beginning of a liturgical season (e.g. Advent, Lent). Again, having something to give to someone makes it easier to describe the opportunity, the value added by participation, and something to hand them in the form of a physical invitation. An example is included below.

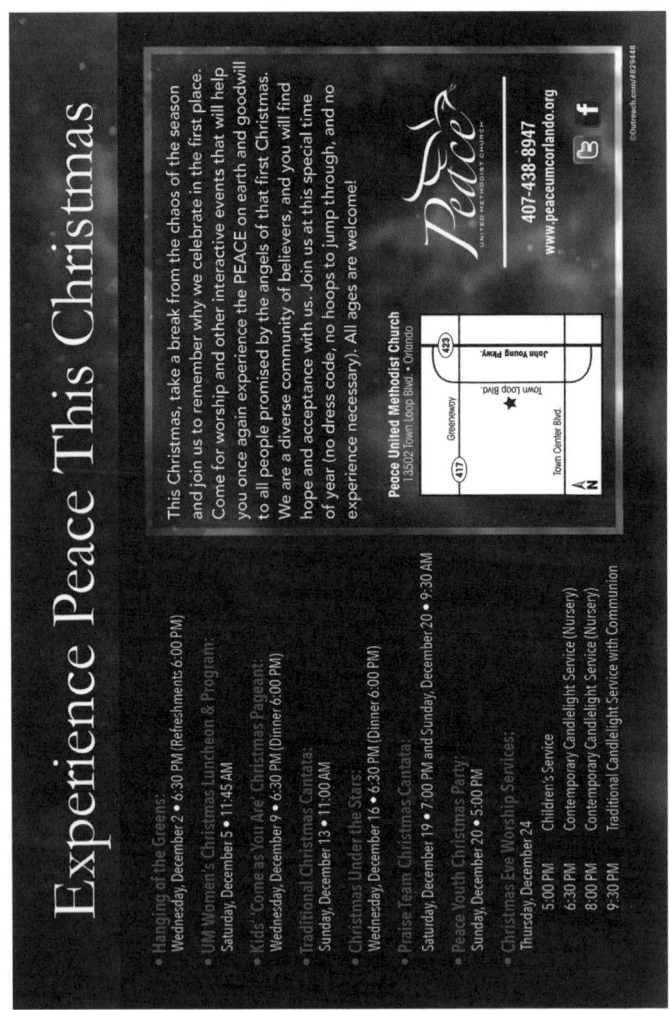

- **The Joe Harding System**: Doug Anderson, in his book, *The Race to Reach Out*, shares a seasonal approach used by Joe Harding:

  o A few weeks before the invitational focus of the season, 3x5 cards are distributed to the congregation.

  o Each participant is asked to write down the names of five people they would like to see come to worship.

  o Participants are encouraged to take the cards home and display them in a prominent place where they would be reminded to pray daily for the people named on the cards.

  o A couple of weeks prior to the invitational focus event, participants are encouraged to extend an invitation.

  o In worship the participants are asked to, by a show of hands, be accountable for praying for and making the invitation. [10]

The result was an increase of 50% on these invitational Sundays and a congregation that experienced significant long-term growth.

- **Special Events/Attractional Ministries**: This refers to the types of events that serve to "attract" people to a congregation through providing visibility and interactions with the local community. Oftentimes, these are identified as "outreach," but this can be a misnomer since most of them are done on church properties—perhaps they are better described as "inreach." These events include things like fall festivals, Trunk-or-Treats (a Halloween gathering in the parking lot with candy distributed from decorated car trunks), Vacation Bible School, pumpkin patches, Christmas tree sales, block parties, concerts, yard sales, and the like. Sometimes these events get a bad rap and are discouraged. They can definitely be great events (especially if other community groups are

"THERE HAVE BEEN MANY 'THANK YOU JESUS' TIMES IN MY LIFE. I WAS 8 YEARS OLD **WHEN I FIRST LOVED JESUS.**"

- PAT, LINE STREET UNITED METHODIST CHURCH

invited to partner with them), but rarely are they a satisfying substitute for actually going out into the community. It's a "both-and" deal rather than an "either-or." The real value of any of these events (other than raising money) is that they are an opportunity for the building of relationships. By this we do not mean merely an opportunity for handing out church brochures. If the church is going to host an attractional event, there should be significant thought given to how the event can build contacts for the congregation (getting names, addresses, and emails), with the goal that these contacts will not merely be used for marketing, but to encourage congregation members to authentically engage those who come from the community.

A word of caution is in order here: it is often the case that congregations get worn out and distracted doing event after event. The result is that they don't have the time or energy to actually go into the community and make a difference. We recommend that these kids of activities be very limited (1–2 per year) to make space for more ministry of engagement.

- **Websites:** Research indicates that as many as 90% of people will visit a church's website before making a decision to attend. That's huge! The following are some suggestions for supporting incarnational hospitality efforts by the congregation through your website:

    o Invest the resources to create a professional-looking site. The quality of your website is considered a reflection of the excellence with which you do ministry.

    o Keep the website current.

    o Have worship times clearly identified with a description of the style of worship offered.

    o Provide clear directions to your church location. Many websites now include a link to MapQuest, Google

Maps, or another mapping tool.

- o Provide information about childcare, emphasizing safety within your childcare ministries; without this, you may lose young families. This includes childcare for special events.

- o Include information about your staff. The best sites even include a personal statement from staff members.

- o Include a place to listen or watch current messages from worship service.

- o Share stories about lives that are changed and the difference the church is making in the community.

- o Include pictures of people engaging other people— in worship, at play, while serving others. Please don't include a picture of your church building unless your claim to fame as a church is being a historical site on the national registry!

- o Make sure that your website is optimized for mobile platforms. Increasingly, the majority of people are accessing websites through smartphones and tablets. If your website is clunky and difficult to use in these formats, people will quickly give up and abandon it.

- **Social Media**: Phil walked into a church recently that had a big banner immediately in front of the doors to the church that stated, "Let All Mortal Flesh Keep Silence." It was no surprise that the pastor, in the opening greeting, asked the congregation to take out their cell phones and place them on "silent" or "stun." He said it as a joke, but the meaning was clear. Contrast that with a recent worship experience at a church in Louisiana where the Worship Leader asked everyone to take out their cell phones (Phil was ready for the 'switch 'em off' admonition related above), but, instead, she asked them to type in the link projected on the video screen at the front of the sanctuary. She then asked everyone to send the link to a friend or colleague and invite them to join in worship through a live stream experience.

Guess which of those churches has experienced phenomenal growth over the years. What if we embraced interactive technology instead of considering the enemy of the worship experience?

o What if participants in worship were encouraged to take a picture of worship happening and encourage their friends to join in?

o What if the church provided a prepared post with great images that members could like and post on their own Facebook pages and use as a tool to invite their friends to join them?

o What if, during the message, an occasional slide would come up with a 140-character quote participants could tweet?

o What if participants in worship, at the time of corporate prayer, were invited to take out their phones and text someone to let them know they were being prayed for during worship that day?

We have seen all of these and many more applications for social media used in local congregations. People rely on these tools in every other dimension of their lives, why not use them to bring glory to God?

It is a natural thing to share with our family and friends and neighbors and acquaintances the things that we enjoy and the things that bring value to our lives. Incarnational Hospitality is simply applying that natural tendency to our spiritual lives as well. It doesn't have to be difficult. It doesn't have to be overwhelming. It doesn't take doctoral level training, ninja skills, or even the spiritual gift of evangelism.

Everyone can do this. And everyone can encourage their local body of believers to make it a priority.

Questions and Exercises for Individuals

1. Are you a booster for your home church? What are three things that you most love telling other people about when describing your congregation? Are there any things about your church that would make you hesitant to invite others?

2. Do you think people see your life as a signpost to Jesus? What are the things they see in you that are overt reflections of God's grace? What habits or attitudes might you change if you were more routinely thoughtful about people perceiving you as Christ's representative?

3. When is the last time you personally invited someone to church? What were the circumstances? When was the last time you had an opportunity to invite someone to church, but chickened out? Why?

4. Revisit the Circle of Influence exercise on pages 80 and 81. Did this exercise change the way that you think about the people whose paths you cross on a regular basis?

5. Looking again at the Circle of Influence exercise and thinking about Alan Hirsch's comments on presence and proximity, are there ways you could be more intentionally present for people?

More actively engaged in their lives? What worries you the most about being engaged in this manner?

6. Who are the people (either types of people or specific individuals) that you have the most trouble accepting and forgiving? How does this reluctance to accept or forgive create distance between you and them?

7. Add to the list of 'thin places' on pages 85 and 86.

8. Do you have tools, props, or supplementary materials for telling your story to others or inviting them to join you? Which of the things listed on pages 91 - 96 would be most useful to you? Can you think of other ideas that might work particularly well for your local context?

9. What kinds of social media do you use on a daily basis? Make a list of the ways you could use social media and the Internet to engage, invite, and encourage people in the ways we have been discussing in this chapter.

Discussion and Activities for Small Group Settings

In addition to comparing your individual responses to the questions in the preceding pages, as well as the group activities suggested within the chapter, give some thoughts to the more institutionally oriented questions below.

1. How does your church help people live differently because of their relationship with Jesus?

2. What are some places in your local community that you would identify as 'thin places'? Would members of the general community recognize these as special places as well?

3. How could we help people become more comfortable in sharing their stories and inviting others to become disciples of Jesus?

4. What sorts of invitational aids does your church offer? What types of resources in this regard would you like to see? Whose responsibility do you think it is to come up with such resources?

• CHAPTER 4 •
ENGAGING THE COMMUNITY

Jesus said, "The harvest is plentiful but the workers are few." (Luke 10:2)   Sometimes we dismiss this statement as pertinent only to the time in which Jesus lived and did ministry. It seems outdated when applied to the conditions of our current culture. We say things like:

• "Everybody in my community already goes to church."

Or, if we are from a Protestant denomination, we might say . . .

• "Everybody in my community is Catholic." (Nothing wrong with that, of course, but it's really just a different version of the first statement).

Or, if we are feeling discouraged, we might say . . .

• "Nobody seems very interested in church in my community."

When we are working with church leaders throughout the U.S., these are common answers to the question of why more people aren't in church on Sunday mornings. But it turns out that only one of these oft-repeated statements actually has any validity. That is why this third statement—the one that turns out to be verifiably true— will be the focus of this chapter on engaging our communities.

But first, let's debunk bullet-pointed responses one and two, because it turns out that they are simply inaccurate. The reality is that in any given community or zip code in the United States, somewhere between 50-70% of the residents have no affiliation to any faith community. They don't have ANY connection whatsoever to . . .

102

- Mainline traditional churches (Methodist, Episcopalian, Baptist, Presbyterian, etc.)
- The Catholic church
- Non-denominational churches
- Jewish synagogues
- Muslim mosques
- Hindu or Buddhist temples

None.

The Quad Report, a detailed statistical analysis available through the research company, MissionInsite, is a great resource to help your leadership team see the reality of this in your own community. [1]

Ah, but that third comment, "Nobody seems very interested in church in my community," is another matter altogether. In all likelihood, if you live in the United States of America, that statement is right on target. And it doesn't really matter what region of the country you call home, what the economic situation is like for local businesses, or what the cultural context is for your unique neighborhood.

The fastest increasing category of stated religious affiliation in America is NONE.

That's right. An increasingly large percentage of Americans are identifying themselves as unconnected with any church at all. For example, *The Pew Research Center* notes:

> The religiously unaffiliated population—including all of its constituent subgroups—has grown rapidly as a share of the overall U.S. population. The share of self-identified atheists has nearly doubled in size since 2007, from 1.6% to 3.1%. Agnostics have grown from 2.4% to 4.0%. And those who describe their religion as "nothing in particular" have swelled from 12.1% to 15.8% of the adult population since 2007. Overall, the religious "nones" have grown from 16.1% to 22.8% of the population in the past seven years. [2]

It is pretty clear that not everyone already goes to church or is a participating member of some other denomination or faith practice. Indeed, it turns out that, just as Jesus said, the harvest is plentiful after all.

The workers, however, are still few—that part has not changed either.

So, how do we, the professed disciples of Jesus—self-identified work-ers—engage the larger community in ways that invite the 'nones' to discover the 'something' in Jesus that is transforming our lives? Perhaps a good starting point is to capture the essence of this very insightful statement by Lovett Weems: **"We have to earn the right to be heard."** In the midst of a cacophony of noise bombarding us every moment of every day, a game plan of standing on the street corner and shouting the Gospel message at the top of our lungs simply places us in the stream of thousands of other suspect messages. So, how do we gain entry into the conversation? How do we earn the right to be heard?

Connecting with the Disconnected

Meet Ben. Ben is a character who appears from time to time in Eddie's neighborhood, looking for small yardwork jobs to pick up some extra cash. He is middle-aged, a little beat up around the edges, lean and laconic, sun-burnt and stubbled. You wouldn't be surprised to hear he had just disembarked from a tramp steamer via Shanghai or returned from a three-month hike on the Appalachian Trail. He'll trim some hedges for you (does a nice job) then disappear for weeks, at which point you might randomly see him pedaling an old BMX bike up the sidewalk a few streets over.

Ben is like a multitude of people we have the opportunity to connect with every single day of our lives. Alan Hirsch, in his book *Right Here Right Now*, co-authored with Lance Ford, describes them as "Extras":

All movies and television shows have them. They are

peripheral to the real action and focus of the camera, which is on the star or main characters, and you don't know their names, backgrounds, or body of work. You've probably never seen them before and most likely will never see them again. They are referred to as extras: basically they are human scenery. These are the people who sit at the tables in restaurant scenes looking as if they are chatting; they play the role of passerby on the sidewalk and the ones who are felled or blown up in battle scenes. . . .

Our lives are filled with "extras." Each and every day as we venture from the seclusion of our homes, we encounter them. The lady pumping gas in the next stall, the construction workers eating lunch on the tailgate of their pickup, the elderly gentleman pushing the shopping cart along the bread aisle. These are common examples of those we pass by and intermingle with every day paying virtually no attention to. They are but background scenery to the main story line. . . . [3]

Consider the following simple activity.

An ancient spiritual exercise, called a Prayer of Consciousness, provides a great way to develop an awareness of how God has been at work throughout your day and how you have responded to that working of God in the details of your life, moments that captured the essence of the kingdom of God and opportunities that were missed. In the traditional format, one spends some time in reflection, thinking through the day just completed (imagine a digital recording of your whole day, ready for review). Where have you seen God at work? At the conclusion of this prayer time, you give thanks for the many ways God was present to you.

The following version of this exercise uses the format of the Prayer of Consciousness to help us develop an awareness of opportunities God has placed in our path to connect with people in meaningful ways. Write down names or descriptions of people you had some contact with. For example: the server at the restaurant or cashier at the grocery store.

8 a.m.	1 p.m.
9 a.m.	2 p.m.
10 a.m.	3 p.m.
11 a.m.	4 p.m.
12:00 p.m.	5 p.m.

(Include more time slots as needed.)

For reflection: What are some specific ways we might connect with these "extras" in a more meaningful way?

Mike is a longtime friend that Phil meets occasionally for lunch. Phil really enjoys these get-togethers. They find a place with good food and usually have some great conversation. But one of the things he likes most about going to lunch with Mike is that Mike never misses an opportunity to engage the server. First he gets their name and then calls them by name each time he interacts with them. Then, as the meals are served, he says, "My friend and I are going to offer a prayer before our meal. Is there anything we can pray about for you?"

Phil notes that, while it is bound to happen sometime, to date he has never seen anyone turn down the opportunity to be prayed for. Some of the things they have prayed about in response to this simple opportunity offered to servers:

- Broken relationships
- Health concerns
- Financial problems
- Children struggling with addictions

It's a terrific witness to connecting in a meaningful way with someone who would typically be an "extra" for most of us.

Speaking of restaurants and servers, we want to encourage you to help Christians (the broader demographic group) overcome a negative image. This became a cause of concern as a result of a conversation with a server from a Cracker Barrel restaurant who made the comment that she didn't like working on Sundays. It wasn't that it took her away from church activities (her father was a pastor). It was because the people who came in on Sundays—particularly the 'after-church' crowd—were cheap. By this she meant that they didn't tip well, or sometimes they didn't even tip at all. They were also the most demanding customers. We have an opportunity to correct this image. We are called to be a generous people, in both our resources and the extension of our patience and empathy. We are blessed to be a blessing.

Become known as a 'great tipper' and see what doors are opened to you!

The opportunities are as broad as our imaginations when it comes to connecting with the "extras." A while back, Phil was observing the crew of men that keep his yard mowed and edged and his trees trimmed, and speculated that they probably moved through the day with little connection to the people for whom they routinely did this labor. Watching them work one day in the hot sun and thinking about the casual anonymity of their efforts, he decided to offer them a cold water break in the shade of his deck (sounds oddly biblical doesn't it?). The owner and he began to have regular conversations, and Phil soon discovered the landscaping boss was a part-time pastor at an independent African-American church. Phil gave him a copy of his first book, *Shift*, and this led to many fruitful conversations. The part-time pastor/full-time landscaper ended up inviting Phil and Becky to his wedding, and later, when Becky was going through chemotherapy, this newly connected friend laid hands on her and prayed for her complete healing.

All because Phil took the time to make a connection with the lawn guy.

"JESUS IS THE REASON I AM SAVED, BECAUSE WITHOUT HIM, THIS WORLD WOULD BE FULL OF DARKNESS. HIS LIGHT STILL SHINES THROUGHOUT THIS WORLD AND IN MY HEART EVERY DAY BECAUSE OF WHAT HE DID ON THE CROSS."

- TANNER, WEST DISTRICT, CTX CONF. UNITED METHODIST CHURCH

Each of us is constantly making casual connections as we go about the business of our day. When working with rooms full of people during leadership seminars, we love to have them do the following exercise. We have each person identify three local businesses that know them (personally) by name. For example, when Phil goes to the cleaners, the associate at the desk (there are several) says something to the effect of "Hi Mr. Maynard. Let me get your clothes." They know him because he is a regular customer and has taken the time to chat them up whenever he stops by. Eddie doesn't have clothes worthy of a visit to the cleaners, but he is definitely on a first-name basis with the servers at several breakfast diners within a few miles of his house.

Those are the kinds of casual but constant relationships which we find ourselves prompting workshop participants to think about as we have them three local business that know them by name. We have them write the name of each separate business on a Post-it note. Then all these individual Post-it notes are placed on a wall, whiteboard, or newsprint so that everyone can see them as a group together. The visual impact is worth the work, because it turns out there are always a surprising number of businesses that already know these church leaders by name. As we consider this spread of Post-it notes, the first question we ask is, "How many of you had trouble coming up with a business that knew you by name?" There are generally a few folks in this category. With some good-natured chiding, we remind these recluses of the opportunities they are missing to make such connections. Then we also take a look at the wide variety of businesses (numbers and types) that are represented.

It's a visual reminder that moving through the world as a human being involves countless interactions. It's unavoidable (and who would want to avoid them anyway—they are one of the revelatory blessings of life—Jesus certainly sought them out at every turn). There is a difference, however, between a quick, mindless interaction and the thoughtful practice of making a memorable connection.

Think about your own responses in the exercise above—and if you are working through this material with a small group, definitely do this entire exercise within your group. Then multiply the possible connections by the number of people in your congregation, and you'll begin to see the exponential possibilities. It is also important to keep in mind that these businesses that have been the focus of our exercise are businesses that care about the community as much as we do, and as much as our church does. They are, in fact, critical partners in the health of our communities. They have invested themselves in the community. In fact, many of the smaller business owners have used their entire life savings to do so. What happens in the community matters deeply to these people. This means that these business owners are natural allies for the good work we disciples want to do to help people live better lives. Many of them are willing partners with the church in activities that will make the community a better place. (Note here that by willing partners we don't just mean that they are eager to donate an item to your youth group silent auction or free ice cream for your last night of VBS—although many will partner with you that way, too, if asked politely. What they are really looking for, however, is a partnership to effect real change and build comprehensive community spirit.)

How do such productive relationships get started? It all begins with making the personal connections.

Who could you bless by making such a connection? How can your congregation develop a greater awareness of this type of opportunity?

Praying for Our Communities

As we lead workshops around the country, we often ask groups about their belief in the power of prayer. Without exception, all of them affirm a strong belief that prayer makes a difference in people's lives. It is also true, without exception, that every church we encounter is seeking ways to reach new people, more people, more diverse people, and younger people. Yet there seems to be a gap between what we say we believe and what we do in regard to prayer (one of perhaps many gaps between what we say we believe and how we choose to act). As we visit worship services with congregations all around the country and listen to the prayers that are offered in church settings (either corporate or individual petitions), rarely do we hear prayers offered for those who do not yet know how much God loves them. We rarely hear prayers that ask God to support those who serve in the community (police, firefighters, local government, homeowners associations, school teachers/administrators, trash collectors). We don't even hear very many prayers about issues that the community might be facing (gangs, drugs, prostitution, broken families, economic hardship). What we most often experience are petitions for the blessing of our in-house ministries, workers in those ministries, and the needs being experienced by the members of our church.

Perhaps the "Prayers of the People" from the United Methodist Order for Morning Praise and Prayer could serve as a reminder of a broader focus:

Together, let us pray for

the people of this congregation . . .
those who suffer and those in trouble . . .
the concerns of this local community . . .
the world, its people, and its leaders . . .
the church universal—its leaders, its members, and its mission . . .
the communion of saints. [4]

What if we, as a people who claim the power of prayer, prayed for our communities, our community leaders, those who serve us, and those in need? Would it make a difference? Rick Rusaw and Eric Swanson, in *The Externally Focused Church,* share the story of Adam Hamilton at the Church of the Resurrection and that congregation's rediscovery of the power of outwardly based prayer:

[Hamilton] also had cards available, addressed to every employee of the Kansas City School District—all 5,700 of them. He challenged each person in attendance (approximately 5,700 people) to take a card, to pray for the person named on it, and, as God would lead, to write a note of encouragement and thanks to that teacher, administrator, custodian, or cafeteria worker. The cards weren't bulk-mailed from the church; rather, each person addressed and stamped a personal letter and included a personal return address on the envelope. Many included their phone numbers and offers to help.

The response of the teachers and staff was tremendous. They were overwhelmed by the encouragement and offers of support. Many contacted individuals, and as a result, many members of the Church of the Resurrection are now involved in tutoring and reading programs in inner-city schools. Church of the Resurrection figured out a simple way to be a blessing to its community. This stuff is not rocket science. Any church of any size can be a blessing. [5]

There is power in prayer.

While Phil was spending a weekend with a new church plant in North Carolina that he was advising, Phil encountered a man who couldn't wait to share his story. At the end of worship, he sought Phil out to describe his transition from being a Jehovah's Witness to becoming a leader in a United Methodist congregation and helping others discover Jesus. The man's story was all about prayer. His wife and her sisters had begun to pray for God to work in his heart—to help him find a real discipleship relation with Jesus, and it took years of faithful prayer on their end, but, miraculously, it happened! (We invite you to visit our website at www.emc3coaching.com and click on the Resources tab in order to hear the testimony for yourselves.) Let stories like this serve as encouragement for all who long to help a loved one or friend find a relationship with Jesus, but who are frustrated and want to give up. Persistence pays off. Sometimes it's like the way a recipe has to simmer for a good, long while rather than be speed-cooked in a microwave.

We often have congregations participate in an exercise in which they create an evocative visual for considering the possibilities of this kind of prayer. Each person in worship is given five Post-it notes (you can tell how much Phil loves Post-it notes). They are asked to write down the names five people who meet the following criteria (one on each of the separate Post-it notes—first names will do):

- This person is not a member of this congregation.
- This person does not appear to be active in any congregation.
- This person is not in your immediate family.
- This person lives in the same city/locale/area as the church is located.

Participants are then invited to place their Post-it notes on a wall. Imagine a congregation of 100 seeing 500 names on the wall, or a congregation of 200 seeing 1,000 such names posted. The effect is dramatic!

Standing there, face-to-face with this panorama of potential prayer, I ask the congregation what could happen if:

- We, as a congregation, committed to pray for these people?

- Doors (or windows) were opened for us to share our faith story and invite them to discover theirs?

- You were to pray, starting today, for the five persons you identified? Do you believe they would be blessed?

- You focused a little less on your daily challenges and desires and a little more on the identified persons? Would you be blessed?

- Just one of the five were to respond to the prompting of God and your invitation?

Would the people involved be blessed? Would the church as an institution be blessed? Would the community be blessed?

Another way to encourage prayer for our communities is to engage in what are called Prayer Walks. Coach Cheri Holdridge describes the practice this way:

When we decide to Prayer Walk as individuals or as communities of faith, we are seeking to connect in a deeper way with the communities in which we live, and we are inviting God to speak to us. We are asking God to show us what we have failed to see. We are asking God to give us new eyes to see what has become invisible to us over time, and new ears to hear what has become 'white noise' to us.

The act of walking gives our bodies something to do. The walking is a sort of calming distraction so that our minds and our souls can focus on listening to God. [6]

Cheri has prepared a guide to conducting Prayer Walks. A copy of this guide (included with her permission) is found in the appendices of this book. We strongly encourage you to try it out—combining an evening walk with silent prayer for the homes and people you pass is healthy physically and spiritually. It is also a productive discipline of gratitude and a great reducer of stress.

If you commit to this practice for a week or two, you might be amazed at what you discover. And even more amazing is the collective impact such behavior can have when an entire congregation takes it on as a project. Challenge your friends in faith to do just that.

Becoming Involved in our Communities

We sometimes get the idea that church is the place and at the time when and where the disciples—that's us—are gathered together. In fact, it is really just the opposite. **Church really begins when the disciples—we, the followers of Christ—are dispersed.**

The hand motions that go along with the little ditty, "Here's the church and here's the steeple, open the doors and see all the people," simply get it wrong. The church isn't the people in the building. The church is about disciples in the community. Influencing the community. Transforming the community. Bearing witness to the Kingdom of God at hand.

What if we were the church—scattered?

- What if we stopped complaining about sports teams scheduling games and practices that conflict with 'our' schedule (as if the church and Sunday were protected like in the days of the 'blue laws' of decades ago)?

- What if, instead, we sent our members to serve as coaches, chaperones, sponsors, and team parents?

- What if instead of bemoaning the fact that our schools are underfunded and understaffed and struggling to provide a quality education, we sent our members to serve as teachers' aides and tutors and playground support?

- What if we saw every community organization (e.g. Rotary or Kiwanis or Lions) as an opportunity to get to know community leaders and support the good work that is being done through their members?

- What if instead of just providing space for Scouting organizations to use for meetings, we saw this as a ministry opportunity to provide leadership and make a difference in the lives of boys and girls?

- What if we were to support community leaders by helping organize the July 4th parade, and we had a float in the parade and provided refreshments?

- What if one of our members or pastor served as the Chaplain for the High School football team?

The opportunities are endless. These are all ways of being in ministry with our communities. And they are all ways of engaging the community relationally to be the presence of Christ and invite others to discover God's love through our witness. Reggie McNeal suggests that we need to change the scorecard when it comes to what we measure as being 'the church.' He argues that we need to move from a member culture to a missional culture:

> Moving from a member to a missionary culture means making heroes of Jesus followers who are using their life assignments as missionary posts to bless people. The idea is that in their daily lives and daily routines, in their relationships and social networks, in their fields of influence, the people of God represent God to people and people to God. This is the work of priests. In a culture that doesn't know the gospel, it is the work of missionary priests. [7]

If the church wants the community to be transformed, we must be involved as transforming agents. To do that might require that we change the questions we are asking. Val Hastings, pastor and coach, writes:

> I heard a statement on the radio that stopped me cold: History changed when a single question changed; when we stopped asking, "How do we get to the water?" and started asking, "How do we get the water to us?"

> What a radical shift for us as human beings!

> My thoughts went immediately to how this relates to us in ministry. How would our churches change if we were to change our questions? [8]

Too often the church asks the wrong questions: questions like, "How do we get more people to come to church?" Perhaps we ought to be asking, "What ways could we make a difference by engaging our community?" Instead of measuring our success by getting people into the church (building), what if we measured our effectiveness as disciples by how many ways we get the church (us) to the people? Of course, some congregations have already been working in that direction. Here's just a sampling of some of the ideas they have generated:

- **New Mover Contacts**: There are a wide variety of organizations that will provide your congregation with a listing of families moving into the area. These are usually very inexpensive. The usual approach for churches using this information (primarily new church plants in our experience) is to send a welcome card and invite people to check out your church. But what if, in keeping with our focus on incarnational hospitality, representatives from the church living in the community actually made a personal contact, took a treat, helped with move-in tasks, and, in general, expressed genuine interested in welcoming them to the neighborhood?

Would you be willing to write a personal postcard of greeting to a new family moving into the community where your church is located? Would you be willing to act as a navigational guide to help those new residents get comfortable in their new environment?

• **Welcome Wagon**: It's an old concept, but still worth the effort. Using the new mover contact information, have representatives from the congregation deliver a 'welcome gift'. It could include coupons for free or discounted services from local businesses, information about your church, or listings of contact information for basic services needed by every new resident to the community.

Would you be willing to be part of a team to contact local business and help put such a welcome basket together? Would you be willing to personally deliver a basket of welcome goodies?

• **Team Support for Community Events**: Most communities host parades, children's days at the park, downtown farmer's markets, arts and crafts shows, and fundraisers for organizations like Relay for Life. Having a team from the congregation supporting these activities is a great way to build relationships and witness to your caring about the community.

Would you be willing to be a community liaison, to help organize or lead a team to have a visible presence at such a community event?

You'll have plenty of other ideas that pop up once you begin a dialogue that is focused in this direction. Each community is different, and each offers unique opportunities. Some things work better some places, other things in others, but the key is to find what is right for you and your community.

Start Something New to Engage Others in the Community

One of the greatest misconceptions in the church is that effective ministry is something that only happens if it is church-sponsored. The advice offered some 30 years ago by now-retired Bishop Dick Willis is still sound guidance. He noted then that a solid, healthy practice for churches was to encourage people to develop their own ministries. If someone had an idea for a ministry and came to talk with him about it, he would ask about how the idea matched up with the vision of the church. If the stated vision and the proposed vision aligned, he would suggest that the person who had approached him with the idea find at least two others with the same passion and go make it happen. No promises for funding or other church support. Just the encouragement to do what God was leading them to do.

I have found that the "**Rule of Five**" is perhaps even a more productive approach. Having five people committed to the start of a new ministry provides a very strong base. Or if you are part of a small congregation, you might instead consider a "**Rule of Three**," remembering the old Ed Mathison quote, "If three people are committed and eager, then let them go, but if you can't find three people, the answer is 'no.'"

Do you hear that quiet whisper of the Holy Spirit prompting you to begin a ministry or outreach? Do you know someone else who is receiving such promptings for whom you might help complete their 'Rule of Five'?

If you want to personally challenge yourself to explore how you might engage people outside the church, you should start with something you, yourself, are really interested in or drawn to. At the church where Eddie serves, they recently launched a Special Needs Ministry. This ministry came to fruition because one man had a daughter with special needs. Her unique condition made it difficult for her to participate in Sunday morning worship, but his vision was that she and others like her, along with their families, would be able to find a significant way to connect with the life of the church. He was bold enough to articulate this vision to Children's and Family leadership, and a team was formed to research existing special needs ministries and resources. It was not an easy task, particularly for a church with limited facilities, but it turned out there was a group of people who were energized by this potential ministry and willing to commit to make it happen (and by the way, this team was formed primarily of people who had not been otherwise motivated by existing ministries).

It doesn't have to be a complex vision or a complicated program. Pre-school parents wanting to have some adult conversation with others in the same circumstance can start a 'play-date' with other parents. Such a group could gather at a local fast food restaurant with a play area or at a local park. There doesn't need to be an agenda. Just some adult conversation and some relationship building. And the resulting interactions don't have to be overtly churchy. The topics of faith and religion just seem to come up naturally when the right setting is provided. One new church planter we worked with actually started an entirely new congregation by steadily building relationships in exactly this manner.

If you are a business person or professional, you will definitely want to explore how faith and religious teachings might impact the workplace in positive ways. You could even begin a weekly lunchtime Bible Study or conversation. Lots of great resources are available to help undertake such activities in an open and respectful environment.

If you're retired, you might get connected with a group of retirees with active minds who enjoy meaningful discussions and an exchange of ideas. You might start a book club, a philosophy club, a TED Talk club (where you watch TED Talks and then analyze their ideas). You might assemble a watercolor painters group, master gardeners, bird watchers, or movie buffs. The possibilities are limited only by our imaginations and our receptivity to the leading of the Spirit.

If you are interested in leading a new thing at your old church, you can be part of a movement to host more freeform worship and fellowship that engages the community with more conversation and less of the conventions of traditional worship. There are even tools for a more organized and structured approach to such gatherings, with standardized curriculum resources like Lifetree Café:

> *"Lifetree Café is a casual and welcoming "conversation café" where great discussion is served up every week. . . . Every week, Lifetree Café gathers friendly people to experience the intriguing stories of life around us. Lifetree is a great place to see old friends and meet new ones."* [9]

One of the pastors Phil partners with as a coach has used this tool to start a second campus for his church and is now doing it again to start a third campus.

Influencing Our Communities

A friend of Phil's who made a move several years ago had two middle school age daughters. One of the first things he did when getting settled into his new job and his new home was join the Parent Teacher Organization (PTO) at the school. Phil was intrigued by this priority, since he had to admit that probably would not have been at the top of his list of things to do. When Phil asked the pastor friend about it, his friend replied, "I want to have a voice in the things that will impact my children." If we want to make a difference, we have to get involved.

A church in a community near Ft. Lauderdale, Florida was frustrated that some of its members and many in the community were getting fined by the city for not having lawns mowed to a particular height or because they had some visible defect on the exterior of their home like shutters missing or broken porch railings. For a few months, the church focused intensely on helping out its neighbors by making these repairs or mowing those lawns. Many in the neighborhood were elderly and/or disabled in some way, so it was an outreach that was welcomed, and on the strength of this popular approach, the church decided to take it a step further. They decided to get involved with the community government. They partnered with other churches in the area and began to attend city commission meetings and address the larger issues.

Eventually they were able to get the city to change this particular ordinance and look for ways to provide assistance to those in need, rather than automatically punishing them. The church focus moved from acts of mercy to justice ministries, and ultimately influenced the actions of local government. Dr. Joseph Daniels with Christie Latona, in a book titled *The Power of Real: Changing Lives, Changing Churches, Changing Communities*, provides the following insights:

Communities work through the interaction and interplay of three basic sectors: public, private, government.

The private sector is the economic engine of a community . . . [and] infuses a community with revenues and jobs.

The governmental sector provides law, order, and services. . . .

The public sector is made up of people who live in a given community and community organizations. . . .

The church should be a major player in the public, private, and governmental sector as the organizer and catalyst for community wholeness in your neighborhoods. [emphasis added] [10]

This may sound a little scary for the great percentage of clergy who are trained in the basics of running a church, not leading a community, but a significant trend in the ministry world today for both new church planters and established congregations is the training provided to become stronger community organizers. Even some seminaries are including this type of training. It's actually a very Wesleyan idea! Remember John Wesley's motto, "The world is my parish"? Even in the 1700s, he saw that much of his ministry was to be outside of the traditional church and would instead involve influencing the world around him. Perhaps it is time to recapture that ideal.

Living into Our Mission

Most United Methodists can quote the Mission of the Church. It's easy and catchy. It has two basic parts:

> Make disciples of Jesus Christ
> for
> the transformation of the World.

Let's take a closer look at the second part of this statement: "For the transformation of the world."

For the vast majority of congregations across the country, this seems to be most routinely interpreted as "doing good" for people or engaging in "acts of mercy". We . . .

- Provide food pantries.
- Provide a hot meal for the homeless in the community each month.
- Give backpacks to children starting school.
- Provide emergency supplies to people in need.
- Prepare peanut butter sandwiches for children who might not have food over the weekend because they rely on school lunches to receive nutrition.
- Distribute gift cards to families that are down on their luck (maybe even pay one of their utility bills on an emergency basis).

- Collect clothes for people who can't afford nice things to wear for a job interview.

All of these things and so many more undertaken by local churches are good things to do, and they are definitely helpful in the moment for the people in need.

But they will NOT transform our communities. The needs will continue to exist the next month or the next week or even the next day, until something happens to change the underlying circumstances.

This is where the transformation of the world stuff comes in.

Transforming the world means that we work to change the systems that create the needs in the first place.

In the previous section, we shared the story of a church that partnered with other churches and convinced the community government to change local ordinances.

Phil was recently inspired by the approach of the leadership of the First United Methodist Church in Eastland, Texas, a congregation with which he had been consulting. This group of leaders decided that if they were going to 'transform' the community, not just meet needs present in the community, it was going to require the church (i.e. people) to become persons of influence. As they talked about what God was already doing in their midst (giving form to their discussion through the use of such workshop tools as asset mapping), it became apparent that God was already providing people of influence. For example, the current City Manager, another person who was a leader in the local child advocacy program, and a third person who served with the public library leadership were already present in the room that day. The group easily identified about 20 other persons who were part of their congregation and already in positions of community influence. The leadership team decided to encourage other members of their faith circle to become involved in greater community leadership at all levels through the development of a Community Partnership Group focused on modeling this kind of engaged leadership.

Think about the transformation that could happen if disciples of Jesus Christ provided leadership for the whole community, not just the church.

Understanding Our Communities

In many of the Districts and Conferences of the United Methodist Church (our denominational tribe), it is now becoming common practice to take the ideal of "the world is my parish" literally. By that, we mean that local pastors are being encouraged to see the scope of their ministry (their "mission field") as being larger than the ministry to those who are formally or informally connected to their specific congregation. They are being asked to see the community as their parish, not just the congregation itself.

This has far-reaching implications and sets up expectations that are different than those many of our clergy have been trained to accomplish. If the church is to be in ministry to the entirety of the community, its effectiveness depends upon developing a more sophisticated understanding about the community in which it is located. We want to suggest several ways to develop such an understanding:

Conduct Community Interviews: If a congregation is going to truly serve the needs of the larger community, it must understand and clearly identify those needs. For example, Phil was in a conversation with a young pastor recently who had discovered through demographic research that nearly 25% of the surrounding community was comprised of single parents. In a fairly typical fashion, conversations began in the church about how to meet the needs of this particular demographic group. One of the church members suggested that they should start an after-school program to provide safe space, tutoring, and even a meal for children of single parents. They were considering starting small (just one day a week) and then expanding as resources became available.

When Phil asked the question, "How could you find out if that is what they really need?" it was like a light bulb went off! This church leader figured it out: "We could ask them!" Instead of projecting what we, the church, think the community needs, it is really helpful to ask the actual people in the community.

A guide for conducting community interviews is included in the appendices.

Community Demographics: A powerful tool for understanding your community is the exploration of your community demographics. A favorite provider of demographic information is MissionInsite. With just a few clicks on your computer keypad to indicate what geographic area you want to define around your church, you can create a QuickInsite Report. In the appendices is a form you can use to help your leadership team process the QuickInsite Report.

One might wonder what this kind of information has to do with Incarnational Hospitality and, specifically, the building of relationships in the community. We would make the argument that, in fact, it has *everything* to do with it.

Incarnational Hospitality is focused on the 'other' person and their needs and perspectives. If the church is going to be hospitable, if we are going to engage people who are not like us, the key is understanding and meeting people where they are. This is very different than expecting people to adapt to what's important and comfortable for us.

The microculture analysis done by author Tom Bandy for Mission-Insite is a great lens into the lives of the people living right around our churches. In the book *See, Know & Serve The People Within Your Reach*, Bandy identifies a variety of alternatives that the church needs to consider when seeking to connect with various lifestyle segments:

- Leadership Alternatives
- `Hospitality Alternatives
- Worship Alternatives

- Education Alternatives
- Small Group Alternatives
- Outreach Alternatives
- Facility and Technology Alternatives
- Stewardship and Financial Management Alternatives
- Communication Alternatives

Bandy offers this example regarding how we as a church community communicate:

> Methods of communication are important because of what they reveal or symbolize about the community and the congregation. The communication techniques have meaning that shape the identity of a local church and how well it is perceived to connect with the community. For example, some lifestyle segments prefer digital technology, while others prefer printed materials. The most common form of communication in churches, even if it is no longer the most common method among many lifestyle segments, is printed materials. People communicate by a variety of ways (print, radio, television, internet, gatherings). Churches need to discern the way the lifestyle segment they are trying to connect with communicates. [11]

Tools like MissionInsite, community interviews (with community leaders/ businesses), Acts 1:8 exercises, congregational interviews, and microculture (lifestyle groups) analysis are really helpful in getting a clearer understanding of the community surrounding the church.

But the real win is people with a heart for the community who are involved in the community and engaging people in the community. Perhaps a goal of every congregation should be to send people out rather than to gather them in. We might just transform the world!

Questions and Exercises for Individuals

1. Look back to the exercise on page 106 (and complete it if you haven't done so already). What insights did you gain by composing this list? Which of the 'extras' that you listed seem like people you might stand the most chance to impact? Make a list here of some people for whom you might be considered an 'extra,' but who have had an impact on you.

2. In two different sections in this chapter, the power of prayer was discussed. How are some ways you could actively integrate prayer into your daily routine? What are some ways you can use prayer to engage others?

3. What did you think of Phil's passionate call for Christians to be better witnesses to the wait staff in restaurants? What are scenes of "bad Christian witness" you have observed personally? How does your role as a disciple influence your dealings with sales staff, servers, and professional people?

4. Based on your own observations, what key words would you use to describe the culture of your community? Imagine that you are writing an article for a travel magazine. In just a few sentences, how would you describe what is unique about your community?

5. What would you describe as the biggest challenges facing your community? What does your community need the most?

6. Looking at the challenges and needs listed in question 5, how could the church of which you are a part lead transformational change in these areas?

Discussion and Activities for Small Group Settings

In addition to comparing your individual responses to the questions in the preceding pages, as well as the group activities suggested within the chapter, give some thoughts to the more institutionally oriented questions below.

1. How well do we model the critical value of connecting and engaging in our community through the activities of worship, gathering events, and the wins we celebrate?

2. What could the leadership of our congregation do to help us really understand the community around us and ways we could engage that community more fully?

3. How could we create a culture in our own congregation of valuing the engagement of the community?

4. How could we encourage participants in our own community of faith to start new things to reach new people?

• CHAPTER 5 •

CONNECTING THROUGH SERVICE

One of Phil's formative experiences early in his ministry was the development of what came to be called the Manna Kitchen at a church he served. It was designed to be a way of serving the large population of homeless persons in the community, and ministering to those who were lonely or living within budget constraints. Manna Kitchen was a Thursday evening meal served in the Fellowship Hall of the church. There was no budget for the meals. They simply served whatever was provided through concerned members and local businesses. It was not unusual to have bread provided by Panera, day old cookies from the Cookie Factory, and trays of macaroni and cheese and coleslaw from Sonny's BBQ. Other nights it might be soups prepared by members or chicken donated by a local butcher.

When they started Manna Kitchen, the leadership team (staff and elected leaders) made a personal commitment to serve dinner to their guests each Thursday evening. After a while, though, one of these leaders had the epiphany that they weren't really getting to know any of the people being served in a deeper way than to say 'welcome' and perhaps 'what is your name'? In the language of Alan Hirsch (whom we heard from in earlier chapters), they were practicing presence, but they weren't fully engaging in proximity.

There were plenty of people who would volunteer to serve the meal, so the staff and leadership switched their role from standing in the serving line to sitting down and eating with the guests. It was an amazing shift! They got to know a lot of details about the lives of many of their dinner guests, and they formed relationships that went well beyond the meal served each week. In effect, Phil became the ex-officio Chaplain to the homeless community. He became the go-to guy when someone was sick or in trouble or just needed some kind of assistance.

And once they felt accepted, valued, and welcomed, many of these guests began to explore participation in worship. Some began to participate in other ministries of the congregation. Later, when Phil moved on to another appointment, a group from the homeless community came to his home and presented him with a new white shirt as a going away gift. It didn't fit, but that didn't really matter. He counts it as one of the treasures from his time in ministry.

We share this account for a couple of reasons. First, because it witnesses to an important part of serving—the building of relationships that have been described throughout this book as Incarnational Hospitality. It would have been a significant ministry to simply feed hungry people. There is certainly plenty of need all around us. But while any organization can take on a project of feeding hungry people (and many noble organizations do), the church is supposed to be more than just a social service agency. We bear witness to the love of Jesus. We feed body *and* soul.

Not, however, in a forced or manipulative way. We've all seen examples of how ineffective those approaches are: for example, the food pantry where the recipients have to be 'counseled' about their relationship with God before they can leave with food. Or the 'free' meal that has a ticket price of having to sit through a 'devotional' time to get fed. What Phil and crew learned from this experience in the Manna Kitchen is the simple power of relationships. They got to know people, and the people got to know them. Two groups of people heard one another's stories. In the words of Henri Nowen:

> It is a privilege to practice this simple ministry of presence . . . still it is not as simple as it seems . . . I wonder . . . if the first things shouldn't be to know people by name, to eat and drink with them, to listen to their stories and tell your own . . . and let them know that you do not simply like them—but truly love them. [1]

The second reason we share this account is that it reminds us about the power of relationships in opening the door to being Christ in people's lives. Really loving people and engaging them in ways that expressed the love of Christ opened the door for connecting at a deeper level. It was risky. It took a lot of time. But the rewards were eternal. The shift from serving a meal to eating a meal with those being served—and taking the time to get involved in their lives—reflected a movement from 'missional gestures' to 'ministries of engagement.'

We encourage all congregations to move beyond missional gestures (which do good and make us feel good) to finding at least one 'ministry of engagement.' In a ministry of engagement, the congregation not only provides resources for those with specific needs, but also has direct contact with those being served. This approach fosters the building of relationships with people so that they may come to know the love of Christ; it engages our hands and feet, rather than just our pocketbooks; and it helps us to grow in our understanding of the needs of those in our community so that we might address both mercy and justice issues.

It is not uncommon to find congregations that are engaged in a wide variety of 'missional gestures,' but have no ministries that provide the opportunity to really engage people in such a way that ongoing relationships are built and the love of Christ witnessed. For example, when working recently with a congregation of a mere 30 active weekly worship participants, this hardy group of disciples was able to enthusiastically identify the following 'service' projects in which they were engaged at some level:

- Bundles of love
- Food distribution
- Community breakfast
- Channel One
- Iowa flooding
- Prayer shawls
- Salvation Army
- Dorothy Day House
- Women's shelter
- Nothing But Nets
- Donation of hats/mittens
- Care Fest
- Christmas and Thanksgiving meals
- Supplies for Habitat for Humanity.
- Teen Challenge
- Nomads

Those were 16 lovingly offered 'service' projects where items were collected and given to local organizations or meals were served, but none of these outreach projects were fulfilled in manner that offered direct, sustained engagement with the people being served. Good was done for sure, but relationships were not being built. This congregation was very generous, but not really engaged in service. Service, we're saying, means we really 'get in there and risk ourselves to serve,' not just give stuff away. We're not suggesting that we shouldn't be generous. Community organizations need our support. But we challenge this congregation and others like it to find a way to move from these 'missional gestures' to at least one 'ministry of engagement' (and many of the above-listed projects, with some thoughtful tweaking, could shift to versions which promote engagement).

Correspondingly, we've encountered some great stories of local congregations which have made this exact leap: from generous ministries without outlets for sustained connection to ministries of generosity which also promote relationship building. First UMC of Hamilton, Texas did just that. They sponsored an effective food pantry that distributed dozens of bags of food every week to people who really needed it (food that was generously donated by congregation members). But they realized they weren't connecting with the people they served—those folks showed up every week, gathered up their donated food, and headed on their way. After prayer and some healthy brainstorming, the Hamilton Methodists started a cooking class, partnering with the county extension agent and using a wonderful cookbook titled, *Good and Cheap: Healthy Cooking on a Food Stamp Budget*. They invited their clients from the food pantry to come join them, and they all got together for class, learning to cook the meals and then sitting down together to enjoy them. Following these impromptu fellowship meals, they would send moms and dads home with the ingredients to make those same meals at home with their families (the very same moms and dad with the very same bags of groceries they had been distributing all along, but this time with a little extra seasoning: the spice of new friendships).

The movement toward really having an impact on our communities can be described by the following graphic, entitled The Graduate

School of Ministry.

Where would you place your congregation's current ministry?

- Systemic Change
- Ministries of Engagement
- Missional Gestures
- Awareness of need of God's call to help
- Oblivious

Where would you place your congregation on this continuum?

Let's consider an example of a congregation moving through this continuum from the book, *Servolution*, by Dino Rizzo, which details the dramatic beginnings of Healing Place Church:

> Our first challenge came the first time I spoke at our new church and twelve people showed up. After I preached, five of them quit. I did the math and figured out if my preaching continued to drop our attendance by 42 percent each service, I had only two more weeks until the place would be empty. [2]

In this initial phase of development, they explored the community to determine needs and God's call to help.

> We were not going to care about the numbers; we would simply do our part to love and serve people, and leave the church growth up to God. We made a game plan for the week ahead that consisted of one major play: do whatever we can to help the people of our community. . . . As soon as we began looking, it was easy to find people who were ready for a servolution, and we started serving them any way we could. [3]

They began with missional gestures, collecting stuff and giving stuff away. Then they moved to deeper ministries of engagement, responding with enthusiasm to meet some of the desperate needs spawned by Hurricane Katrina.

> [A] chain reaction [was] ignited when our sound system fried... So we decided to hold a big garage sale to raise the funds...Just hours before the sale, I received a call from a man who wanted to give an offering to pay for the new sound system. . . . But now we had all this stuff sitting in the parking lot. Since it was all ready anyway, we decided to go ahead with the sale. . . .

> "I can't take this haggling anymore! So I have an idea. Let's just give everything away." [N]ot only did we give everything away, but we made a great impression on the community. . . .

> The chain reaction of our servolution continued as people from our community began to see church in a whole new light and started showing up to services because they wanted to be a part of it. [4]

And in the end, these efforts led to a broader vision and cooperation with other like-minded congregations to solve problems and promote systemic change.

> It was clear to everyone that the job at hand would require far more than any single government, city, or ministry organization could handle alone. We were all going to need to work together. . . .

> More than four hundred and fifty Louisiana churches were already connected through PRC (Pastors Resource Council), a coalition of churches and ministries we had helped form . . . to address social and economic challenges. . . . [5]

The result? Healing Place Church now operates on eight campuses with a weekly worship participation of 6,000. Dino Rizzo has provided leadership for a group of pastors that has now planted and resourced over 135 new churches in 33 states. That's pretty amazing stuff to come out of a commitment of just a few people to give themselves away to the community in service and generosity! While it's an unrealistic expectation that every church will see this kind of result, it does seem clear that engaging people in relationships as we serve them is a great way to introduce people to the one relationship that changes everything. So, if a congregation decided that it wanted to engage the community in such a manner, how might it get started?

Partnerships

We encourage churches to consider partnerships with other organizations as a way to begin the process of getting out into the community to serve and build relationships. Too often, the church seems to think it needs to develop everything from scratch, when there are lots of opportunities around us to partner and have a significant impact.

In Orlando, Florida there is (like in many communities) a two to three-mile stretch of road in a fairly well-off neighborhood where you can find nearly every flavor of religious institution. At one point, each church offered its own separate food pantry ministry to the economically challenged in the area. In an unusual spirit of cooperativeness, these churches got together and realized they could make a greater impact and operate much more efficiently if they were to pool their resources and all support a food pantry in one location. What a concept!

In addition to services that are offered by churches, most communities host a variety of social service and public service organizations that are making a difference in the lives of people. These organizations need the support of people from our churches in order to be effective.

For example, Habitat for Humanity provides housing for low income families through the building of homes where the construction is accomplished by volunteers from the community. Some churches take on the entire project of building a home (usually a large congregation in this case), or churches can partner with each other to take on a Habitat project, or they can simply send small teams to support a community effort in the building of a home. It's a great way to make a difference, build relationships within the church, and connect with people beyond the church's doors.

One of our favorite ways of partnering is when faith communities "Adopt A School." Most local public schools have a variety of needs that can be met by volunteers from congregations. There are great needs due to the financial constraints that school systems face, and volunteers can often fill the gap, providing services where funding is not available to hire staff:

- Classroom volunteers
- Tutoring
- ESL (English as a Second Language) classes
- Playground chaperones
- Field trip chaperones
- Office support
- Teacher aides

And don't forget direct help and support for the teachers, themselves. In one church where Phil served, they partnered with teachers at the beginning of the school year to assist with the 'move-in' day. Teams from the church would help teachers move furniture around, decorate classrooms, and arrange supplies. They also provided lunch for teacher work days, recognized teachers and students during worship at the beginning of the year, and invited them to participate in a service of blessing. At the end of the year, they provided a Teacher Appreciation dinner and blessed the teachers with a great meal and a gift to thank them for their service to the children and families of the community. All of this was in addition to acts of generosity, including the donation of school supplies and backpacks for children in need. At least one Conference in the United Methodist Church has asked every church within that Conference to either sponsor or co-sponsor a local school.

Partnering with a local school also provides great opportunities to build relationships with the children, parents, and teachers. This, of course, opens the door to better understand the needs of families. Sometimes additional opportunities will come up through these interactions to provide training in parenting skills, financial management, general life skills, and even job hunting skills.

There are almost countless opportunities to partner with organizations in most communities and participate where God is already at work:

- Community Patrol
- Victim Advocates
- Family Assistance
- Clothing Distribution
- Thrift Shop
- Executive Support
- Adult Day Visitors
- Childcare
- Suicide Prevention
- Special Advocates
- Hospital Volunteers
- Hospice Volunteers
- Big Brother Big Sister

We encourage congregations, when seeking opportunities to serve, to look for opportunities for maximum engagement and relationship building potential. Dr. Joe Daniels and Christie Latona, in *The Power of Real: Changing Lives, Changing Churches, Changing Communities*, suggest the following criteria when considering a partnership with local organizations:

1. Do they share your vision for the community?

2. Do they have a solid, positive reputation in the community?

3. Do they operate their organization with integrity?

4. Do they have a proven track record of rendering service to community members and to other community organizations?

5. Are they really committed to securing the community's well-being through the services that they deliver? [6]

One of the more 'successful' churches in the United Methodist Church's Florida Conference (in terms of getting people connected in making a difference) is Georgiana UMC on Merritt Island. Phil can remember way back in the day when he was growing up and this church had about 25 people in worship together in a typical white frame church. Now nearly a thousand gather for worship each week, and the vast majority of those people are involved in serving the community in some way. However, almost none of the service opportunities are directly the ministry of the church. This congregation made the decision several years ago to encourage the body of Christ at Georgiana to become engaged in supporting the plethora of organizations already doing amazing ministries in the area (including other churches). On any given weekend and many weekdays, you can find participants in this community of faith giving freely of their time and energies and resources to support good work that is making a difference in people's lives.

Neighborhoods

We love being in conversation with churches describing amazing ministries they are doing on the other side of the world: creating orphanages in Haiti, training local pastors in Zimbabwe, or building community centers in Jamaica, churches in Mexico, or feeding stations in Honduras. These are great ministries that meet real needs and bless people in ways they could have never anticipated. Those same churches, though passionate about foreign mission projects, can sometimes struggle when asked about their ministry/mission in the one to two-mile radius around their church campus. Asking leadership to talk about their local projects of engagement can produce blank stares as a response. Several years ago, Phil and Eddie were serving together in a congregation situated in an area that was crisscrossed by three hurricanes in a period of just a few weeks. Power was out in much of the community. Trees were blown down across driveways and roads, and about one out of every three to four homes had significant loss of roofing shingles and, as a result, were leaking into interior spaces. This congregation decided to do something to help. A team prepared coffee and light meals to deliver to those without power. Other teams went home-to-home tacking down blue tarp over damaged roofs to prevent further damage inside. They even had teams that cranked up their chainsaws and helped clear the roads and driveways so people could get in and out of the community.

It was an amazing realization for this congregation that they had something to offer to the community. Church wasn't just about how the congregation could benefit from worship and ministry. Church was people getting out into the world and making a difference.

With this new understanding, this congregation began an outreach ministry in the community doing yard clean-up, minor repairs, painting, and more. It was an exciting time for the them as they discovered they really have an impact in the immediate community and build lasting relationships at the same time. Some of those families on the receiving end of the help even became involved in the church's ministry. All of them experienced the love of Christ in really practical ways.

A MAJOR ENTRY POINT INTO A COMMUNITY OF FAITH, ESPECIALLY FOR YOUNG ADULTS, IS ENGAGEMENT IN SERVING OTHERS. INVITE YOUR COMMUNITY TO PARTICIPATE!

A congregation in Delaware discovered through its demographic analysis (see previous chapter) that nearly 25% of the families in the surrounding community were single parent households. This awareness spurred discussion around how the church could help this demographic group that was largely disconnected from the church.

A number of great ideas were suggested:

- Parents' night out
- Kids' club
- Big Brothers / Big Sisters
- After-school program

This congregation decided to begin an after-school program with snacks, tutoring, games, and a faith-formation activity. They started small, enrolling about 10 children. Each family committed $1.00 per week, which gave them buy-in and helped it feel less like charity. Retired teachers from the church and community provided the hands-on support.

In a similar vein of practical impact, a church Phil recently visited announced a car maintenance day for single moms. They would be provided an oil change and minor repairs free of charge.

One of the most out-of-the-box examples of connecting with the neighborhood comes from a small United Methodist Church. The average age of the congregation is around 70. It is located in a smaller town. There have not been any young families or children or youth in the church in years. The congregational leadership had noted that there were lots of kids in the neighborhood, and they decided that they wanted to engage them in some way, so they refurbished a run-down basketball court located on the side of the building that had not been used in years. Then they invited the kids to come, and they offered them sodas and snacks while they played. Pretty soon, a handful of youth became more than 20, and the church members decided to invite them inside. They set up a sound system and ping-pong table, and provided refreshments every Friday evening. Sometimes as many as 50 youth now gather at this church of old fogies. It is a great ministry and has brought new life to a previously dying congregation.

What a great example of 'doing whatever it takes'!

The key in connecting through service is that we develop a heart for the people we are serving: a heart that longs for people to know the love of Jesus Christ. Service is not just a bunch of projects that make us feel good about doing something good. It is not a ritual that fulfills some religious expectation.

Service is about engaging people in ways that make a difference in their lives, that build relationships, and that invite them to discover the love of Jesus through us. When we keep that truth at the center of all our efforts, the hard work of relationship building is never done in vain. God will always make good use of our efforts.

Questions and Exercises for Individuals

1. What are community service projects and programs (separate from activities sponsored directly by your church) in which you have been involved? What drew you to these projects? What have you learned from your experiences with them?

2. On page 138 a list of criteria is offered for evaluating community service programs and projects. Make a list of your own personal priorities / requirements for deciding to get involved in a community service project or program.

3. Although our churches can take the lead to fill important gaps in serving our communities, what advantages are offered by being involved in community service that is not directly sponsored by our local church?

4. Make a list of your own examples of effective church / community partnerships.

5. What factors are important in order for such partnerships to prosper?

6. Why is service a fundamental, non-negotiable part of living life as a disciple of Jesus Christ?

CONNECTING THROUGH SERVICE
Discussion and Activities for Small Group Settings

In addition to comparing your individual responses to the questions int he preceding pages, as well as the group activities suggested within the chapter, give some thoughts to the more institutionally oriented questions below.

1. In the space below, list the activities that your congregation commonly calls service or outreach to the community:

2. Circle the activities that provide an opportunity for direct engagement where relationships are built.

3. Is this congregation more focused on missional gestures or ministries of engagement?

4. What are some possibilities for developing a ministry of engagement?

• CHAPTER 6 •
DEVELOPING A PERSONAL FAITH STORY

Preparing and practicing a version of the story of our personal faith journey is an important part of our call to share the Good News with others. Perhaps it seems too forced or artificial to think through and practice our personal story—shouldn't it just spring from us naturally in conversation at the right moment? Most of us who have been disciples for any length of time know that it doesn't work like that. As we are making ourselves open to connections with others and as we are creating opportunities for honest exchanges, the very instant when we get the opportunity to answer a question or share our own story is the very moment when we can become blabbering nincompoops. Words can fail us—we get befuddled and don't say what we mean to say.

The pressure is on. We have reached the window of opportunity for which we have been hoping and praying. The stakes are high, and we desperately want to get it right because we so passionately want to share what God has done for us. We want others to know that same peace and purpose that we have come to know. It's just human nature that we would flounder with so much seemingly at stake.

So, first of all, relax. The beautiful thing about building authentic relationships is that everything doesn't boil down to one climactic moment. This is a key differentiation between the classic evangelism of randomly knocking on doors and the relationship-focused evangelism of cultivating long term connections built on love. We'll have plenty of opportunities for conversations with people, plenty of opportunities to get them directed to our ministry partners who know more than we know and who are perhaps more articulate than we are. But most of all, we have been consistently sharing the Gospel through our actions—our deeds of love are more eloquent than our words may ever be.

Words do matter, however. And if we want our words to be clear and purposeful—to be a coherent reflection of what's in our hearts—it is important to embrace the value of advance preparation and the benefits to be gained from thinking deeply about our own faith stories. Not only does telling our story make us a stronger advocate for the Good News, it also helps us more deeply understand exactly who we are as children of God and who we are called to be as followers of Christ in the world.

It is worth taking a moment to talk about the language we use when we're talking about talking about Jesus. If you have been involved in church for a while (and particularly if you older than 30), you will be familiar with the terms *witness* and *testimony*. These terms, often used interchangeably, are a fundamental part of the evangelical tradition (evangelical referring to, among other things, our belief that we are called to personally share the Good News with others). Presumably, you readers who have made it this far in this book, are evangelical in outlook and eager to share your faith, since this book has been totally about that process.

So, having decided to follow Jesus (discipleship), and excited about sharing Jesus with others (evangelism), we want to be intentional about how we share, and this is where our *witness* or *testimony* come in. Don't let the *Law and Order* legalese intimidate you. We act as witnesses, giving first-hand accounts of what we have experienced. We give our testimony: that is, we speak the truth as we know it. We have used those terms throughout *Connect! For Individuals*, but we are also fond of the phrase personal faith story—it has less baggage associated with it, particularly for those who have not grown up in the church.

A prepared personal faith story is useful in a wide variety of circumstances:

- A well-prepared personal faith story brings flesh and blood reality to every witnessing situation. It provides of evidence of

God at work in your life. (Matthew 5:14-16)

- A well-prepared personal faith story can be used in large groups, small groups, and one-on-one situations.

- It explains through a firsthand narrative—your own unique firsthand narrative—what one needs to know to become a Christian.

- This personally crafted narrative can easily be expanded or shortened based on the time available to share in a given situation.

- While a listener can certainly argue with you endlessly about Scripture and theology, it is difficult (and impolite in most circles) to refute another person's direct experiences.

The words of 1 Peter 3:15, that we first shared in chapter one, give a clear directive to all followers of Christ:

> "But sanctify Christ as Lord in your hearts, always being ready to make a defense to everyone who asks you to give an account of the hope that is in you, yet with gentleness and reverence."

And you will recall that back in chapter two, we shared a strong biblical example of such a personal faith story when we focused on the Apostle Paul's statements in Acts 21 and 22. You are strongly encouraged to go back to that earlier section and read Paul's words carefully. In fact, try reading them aloud (to yourself or in a group setting). Use that stopwatch app on your smartphone and time the reading, noting how it covers so much dramatic territory in such a compact time frame. It perfectly captures Paul's faith transitions, en-capsulating the period before he knew Christ, how he came to know Christ, and how his life changed after he came into a relationship with Christ. In fact, if you take an analytical approach to Paul's story as related in these chapters—that is, if you think about it structurally from a writing or storytelling perspective—you can see that it contains three distinctive sections: a "before" section, a "how" section, and an "after" section. On the many occasions when Paul shares his personal story, he tends to organize it in this manner:

- <u>Before</u>: A general description of his life before he became a believer. (Acts 22:1-5)

- <u>How</u>: An exact description of the manner in which he became a believer. (Acts 22:6-16)

- <u>After</u>: A specific example of how Christ has changed his life (Acts 22:17-21)

Paul's epistles and the personal words of witness he offers within them also provide a great example of how easy (and appropriate) it is to adapt a well-thought-through testimony to a specific audience. Compare his words to a Jewish audience in Acts 22:1-21 and his words to a non-Jewish audience in Acts 26:1-23. In each case, Paul carefully tailors his words and his arguments to the background and interests of his listeners.

This is an encouraging example for us as we consider the specific circumstances in which we may have the opportunity to share our personal faith story. We can adjust the language we use, the particular kinds of stories we tell, and our approach in telling them—more logical and straightforward or more emotional in content—based on who is listening, how long we have to share, and whether we are in an intimate or more public setting. If we know someone is facing a difficult decision, we can make sure and focus on how knowing Christ has impacted our ability to process difficult decisions. If we are dealing with someone who is feeling burned out on bad personal choices, we can focus on how having a relationship with Jesus gave us the power to make healthier choices with more integrity. In each of these scenarios, we can still stick to the "before," "how," and "after" model, but the details will shift dependent on the needs of the moment.

Preparing Your Own Personal Faith Story

For a straightforward approach to developing our own personal faith story (traditionally referred to in evangelical circles as our *testimony* or *witness*), just follow Paul's lead. He has, as we saw in the previous section, given us a clear three-point outline:

1. <u>Before</u>: What was your life like before you received Jesus Christ?

2. <u>How</u>: How did you come to know and/or receive Christ?

3. <u>After</u>: What happened (what changed) in your life after you received Christ?

Up until this point, you've probably been nodding your head in vigorous agreement as to all the wonderful justifications for developing a personal faith story, but right about here, as we get to the practical realization of this worthy goal, is when many people begin to protest that their own particular story is too boring, too average, too blah and unengaging for anyone to be influenced by it. You might say, "Look at Paul's story! Full of drama! Look at all the stories we get in the devotional books we read: the lives of saints and heroes! Who cares about our pedestrian experiences?"

Well, first of all, the person who is asking you the question cares. Maybe he or she is asking you a direct question about your understanding of who God is and who we are in relation to God. More likely, they are asking you how you got through a difficult time. How you learned to be so generous. Or loving. Or filled with integrity. Or hope. What they are asking is how YOU got to be the way YOU are.

They are not looking for an essay on theology. They know YOU. They have been encouraged by YOUR actions of love and YOUR words of encouragement and welcome. YOU have earned credibility with them. So, it's YOUR words that matter.

Secondly, everybody's story has resonance. It is much more likely that your account of day-to-day challenges with balancing priorities and working through the world's call to materialism will resonate with a neighbor or co-worker more than the tale of the adventurer who came to know Jesus escaping an avalanche on Everest (because everybody can relate to that, right?).

Even if your conversion story (how you came to accept Christ) seems mundane to you—even if you attended church with your parents from infancy and you received Christ at an early age—the three point Paul-inspired outline is a solid place to start. You might shift more of the emphasis to your life after you had come to know Christ. You might focus more on those pivotal moments in which your faith was challenged or grew deeper. Perhaps there was a point at which you drifted away from God. Focus more on that part of the story: how you returned to following Christ and what has happened since.

Testimony Preparation Worksheet

Use the following questions to help you develop your unique story.

1. What was your life like before you received Jesus Christ?

   Honest examples will establish you as a credible witness in the minds of non-Christians. Avoid religious terminology (terms like saved, redeemed, etc.). Find a central theme in your life and weave your story around it. General statements are better than detailed explanations. A bird's eye view is what works best here. Avoid being explicit or lurid in speaking of drugs, immorality, sexuality, crime, or other sensational topics. Avoid direct references to a specific church or denomination.

   a. What was my life like? What were my attitudes? My needs? My problems?

b. Around what priorities did my life revolve the most? From what did I get my security, significance, and happiness?

c. How did those areas begin to disappoint me?

d. In what ways were my activities unsatisfying?

2. How did you come to know and make a decision to follow Christ?

a. When and how was the first time you heard the Gospel? (When were you first exposed to authentic Christianity?)

b. When did your attitudes begin to change? Why?

c. What were your initial reactions?

d. What were the final struggles that went through your mind before you accepted Christ?

e. In view of those struggles, why did you decide to accept Christ? What was the deciding factor of the decision process?

f. What exactly was the process of the moment of confession and acceptance for you? What words did you use? (It is important to be as exact as possible in this answer because these words can serve as a model for a person who hears your story and wants to make the same decision for themselves).

3. What happened after you received Christ?

a. What specific changes has following Christ made in your words, actions, and attitudes?

b. How long did it take before you began to notice these

changes in yourself?

c. How would you describe the difference in your motivations now versus the difference in your motivations before you decided to follow Christ?

It is also a good idea to sum up your own story by circling back to the Scriptures to share a verse or two that have been influential for you. What are some key verses from the Bible that have sustained you in your faith walk or best capture your spiritual journey?

Now, take your notes from all of the questions posed in the last few pages and use them as a guide to write out your own faith story on the following three pages. This exercise in actually writing down your story is difficult for many people, but it is a critical step. To quote Edgar V. Roberts, "An unwritten thought is an incomplete thought." Writing your story will help you realize what parts are most important and what parts are extraneous (particularly if you practice sharing it with other people).

DEVELOPING A PERSONAL FAITH STORY

Use this page to write down your BEFORE STORY. This is the story of my life BEFORE Christ:

_____

_____

_____

_____

_____

_____

_____

_____

_____

_____

_____

_____

_____

_____

_____

_____

_____

_____

_____

_____

_____

_____

_____

_____

Use this page to write down your HOW STORY. This is the story of HOW I came to know Christ:

_____

_____

_____

_____

_____

_____

_____

_____

_____

_____

_____

_____

_____

_____

_____

_____

_____

_____

_____

_____

_____

_____

DEVELOPING A PERSONAL FAITH STORY

Use this page to write down your AFTER STORY. This is the story of my life AFTER I decided to follow Christ:

_____

_____

_____

_____

_____

_____

_____

_____

_____

_____

_____

_____

_____

_____

_____

_____

_____

_____

_____

_____

_____

_____

_____

_____

_____

Once you have written down the three "chapters" of your story, you can work at melding them into a seamless narrative. It is important to have a longer version (which will include much of what you have written), but also very important to have a distilled version, sometimes referred to as the "elevator speech."

The "elevator speech" is a succinct statement of why you believe in Jesus. Imagine that you have just enough time to share with someone as you are riding to your floor in an elevator with them. So, let's say a minute, or a minute-and-a-half, maybe. There will be windows of opportunity in your day-to-day life in which you have no longer than that to make an impression on someone. Make those words count. We have included photos and statements of some real-world disciples throughout this manuscript to give you an idea of how people have chosen to summarize their faith. Flip through the book again, pausing on those pages and thinking more strategically about the experiences on which people have chosen to focus, the feelings they have highlighted, and the words they have used.

What is most important to you about your relationship with Jesus? How has Jesus most dramatically impacted your life? Choose your words carefully.

As stated earlier, once you have your personal faith story in print, practice it. This is a great activity to do with a small group. If you have an opportunity to share, share! The more familiar you are with the words and saying them aloud, the more comfortable you will be when the opportunity to speak them arises. When you find yourself with such an opportunity—when you've made that vital connection and someone is curious about why you are the way you are, willing to give generously of yourself in love—remember these things:

- Be yourself. You are not called to be a street preacher, actor, or a defense lawyer for God. (Well, some of you might be called to be either of the first two, but most of you will not be—the key is to be true to who God has called you to be.) It is your personal, relatable experience that counts.

- Don't lecture, threaten, or make people feel bad about who they are. Be encouraging, and offer insights into hope, grace, and forgiveness.

- Don't be offensive or judgmental. Meet people where they are.

- If someone listens to you and tells you they would like to have a relationship with this Jesus whom you follow, have a simple prayer in mind in which you can guide them, and have a plan in mind for connecting them with a spiritual mentor who can help them get started on their journey.

Examples of a Personal Faith Story

Phil's Elevator Speech
"Why I believe in Jesus"

Hi, my name is Phil. It took me a while to get there, and the journey included a couple of U-turns, but I can tell you with great confidence that Jesus can take a life that nobody thought would amount to anything and create a life that that knows the love of God and the transforming power of the Holy Spirit. That is my story. Jesus has taken me from a lifestyle of self-reliance and self-centeredness to discover the joy of a personal relationship with Jesus and sharing His story. I have been blessed and am now joined with Jesus to be a blessing to others.

Phil's Personal Faith Story
(This is the longer version—notice the "before," "how," and "after.")

I grew up in a Christian home where my mother was a church choir director and my dad was very active in church leadership. Whenever the church doors were open, it seemed we were there. I was involved in Sunday School, youth group, youth choir and routinely went to summer youth camps. It would seem to be the ideal foundation for growing toward maturity as a disciple of Jesus Christ. The problem was that the 'church stuff' didn't really translate to home or life stuff. They were separate worlds. So, once I was out on my own, I discovered that I didn't really have the relationship with Jesus that I claimed to have. The religious routines didn't seem to do much for me anymore.

As a young married adult, I took a job across the country, and free from the influences of my family and friends, I pulled away from the church. While my wife and daughter went to church on Sunday mornings, I played racquetball with my new best buddy. I could see no point in going to church, and especially in giving money to the organization. I didn't need that stuff anymore. The truth was that I was pretty caught up in my self-reliance, and didn't really think I needed a relationship with Jesus anymore. The result was that I almost destroyed my marriage and family.

By the time we returned to Florida, my family and I were struggling. Finally, my wife, Becky, convinced me that it would be good for the kids to be involved in church activities, so I agreed reluctantly to accompany them. After a few months I made a recommitment (perhaps the first real commitment) to be a disciple of Jesus—this was the result of some deep conversations with the Pastor and some church members. I even got involved in helping lead youth group and youth choir. It turned out to be an amazing time, as I discovered the transforming power of Jesus. I even got to be part of helping other people discover this same relationship.

Four years later, as I was praying with a couple of youth who were making a commitment to Jesus, God called me to full-time ministry. I left my teaching position at the local University and went to Seminary where I earned an M.Div and Th.M (in Spiritual Formation) and then a D.Min. The last 25 years of my life have been dedicated to helping people discover a life-changing relationship with Jesus and helping churches live into their potential. It has been an amazing ride, and while it has not always been easy, it has always been blessed.

I can't wait to see what God has in store for me next!

Questions for Reflection

1. What was the most difficult aspect of writing your personal faith story?

2. What intimidates you the most about sharing your own personal faith story?

3. What are some scenarios that you can think of, based on your day-to-day experience, in which you might need to adjust your story to better fit a particular audience?

4. What are some of the aspects of your personal faith story with which you think people might most compellingly connect? What are some aspects with which they might be least likely to connect?

5. What are some strategies and techniques for sharing the Good News that you have seen fail? Why?

6. When was the last time you had an opportunity to share your story and felt like you let it get away?

CONCLUSION

This book began as a series of questions: "How do we make meaningful connections beyond the walls of the local church? How do we begin the conversation?"

The organized outposts of faith are experiencing a restlessness. It is disturbing to some and exhilarating to others. No longer are people showing up to church just because that's what is expected of them. Young people are impatient with the explanation of doing things a certain way because of heritage or tradition. Technology is altering our understanding of community and spiritual engagement.

And yet, in the midst of what often feels like chaos to those of us who have spent decades in church leadership, there is a new hunger for the things of God—a fresh and energized reading of the Gospel that takes Jesus' words as a serious challenge to bring God's grace to the world. In that sense, this is a golden time. Although many of our local churches are worried about 'gloom and doom' scenarios, this is an opportunity to earnestly seek the guidance of the Holy Spirit, to focus in on exactly who we are called to be in the communities where we have been called to serve (both as individuals and as organized congregations).

And it is a wonderful age of specialization—within the context of our denominations and their rich histories and robust support systems—there is a growing sense of the importance of adapting our ministries to the particular needs of our local communities. We are not so much a branch of a national chain like Cracker Barrel (whose great attraction is that the décor and menu of every single restaurant is exactly the same as every other). We are a unique subsidiary, grounded in a shared theological outlook, but organic to our own particular cities, towns, villages, and neighborhoods. We are more like the ubiquitous local diner: every breakfast outpost on every highway in America has the same basic plate of eggs and bacon, but the sides are different, as well as the accents of the servers, and the quirky decorations on the walls. All those extras that surround the basic, sustaining meal are delightfully unique to every distinct village and town.

We hope this book has helped you begin the journey of what that means for you and your local church. How are you called to fulfill your unique God-given destiny? We pray that the Holy Spirit richly blesses you as you are intentional about connecting with that community around you—a community that is eager to be loved and eager to experience a message of hope.

God bless you in the good work ahead, and if there's anything we at EMC3 can do to help, just let us know.

- Phil Maynard and Eddie Pipkin

APPENDICES

Strategies for Getting to Know Your Community

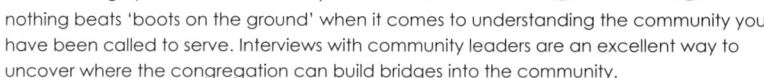

• **CONNECT WITH LOCAL BUSINESSES**

• **COMMUNITY INTERVIEWS**

Preparing for the Community Interviews

Getting to know the community . . . personally!
While demographic studies are a very valuable tool,
nothing beats 'boots on the ground' when it comes to understanding the community you
have been called to serve. Interviews with community leaders are an excellent way to
uncover where the congregation can build bridges into the community.

Who might be helpful to interview? Think of persons who would be able to give you
insights into community trends and needs. Such persons in your community might include:

• **Mayor**

• **Council Representatives**

• **Police Chief**

• **Fire Chief**

• **Home Owners'**
  Association

• **Realtors**

• **School Principals**

• **Hospital Administrators**

• **Social Service agencies**

• **Pastors of other**
  congregations

• **Chamber of Commerce**

• **Neighbors in your**
  community

Who should make the interviews? Involve people in
the interviews who will represent the congregation
well and who will be at ease speaking with
community leaders. It also needs to be people who
are able to ask leading questions and then listen and
learn from what they hear.

Keep the interviews simple: The purpose of the
interview is to listen. After greetings, give a simple
explanation that your congregation is conducting
a series of community leader interviews to discover
ways in which they can be of greater service to
others. Then ask the community leader the following
open-ended questions and let them talk. The first
question is designed to be an easy ice breaker:

• What do you like most about living in this community?
• What are the greatest needs that you see in our
  community?
• How might the church be of service to you and/or the
  community?
• Where do you already see people coming together to
  make good things happen?

Preparing the Community Interviews Summary Report
Since this is a summary report, keep it to no more than one or two pages. After
listing who was interviewed and by whom, briefly share key discoveries around the
following three questions:

• What are the greatest unmet needs in our community?
• Where might our congregation be a blessing to the community?
• Where is God already at work through others that the congregation might
  choose to support?

Strategies for Getting to Know Your Community

Through Demographic Information

- **Run a QuickInsite Demographic report for a 1-mile radius around your church**
- **Complete the following "Exploring Who is in Our Community Exercise"**
- **Identify the top 3-4 Mosaic Groups**
- **Complete the "Uncovering Lifestyle Trends" worksheet**

Exploring Who is in Our Community

Population Trends:

What is the population of your study area? _____

Is the population projected to grow or decline? _____

By what percentage? _____

By how many households? _____

Age Trends:

What is the average age in the community? _____

Is the area growing older or younger? _____

Income Trends:

What is the average household income? _____

Is the average income growing or declining? _____

Generational Trends:

Which group has the largest presence in the area? _____

Which group has the smallest presence? _____

Which group has the greatest growth projected? _____

Which group has the greatest decline projected? _____

Racial/Ethnic Trends:

What is the percentage represented by each racial/ethnic group? _____

Which group has the highest projected growth? _____

Which group is projected to have the greatest decline? _____

Uncovering Lifestyle Trends: *Who are our Neighbors?*

Referring to the people group descriptions just handed out, summarize the characteristics and concerns/needs of the top three people groups in your community.

GROUP: ____ PERCENTAGE: ____ Characteristics: Concerns / Needs:	GROUP: ____ PERCENTAGE: ____ Characteristics: Concerns / Needs:	GROUP: ____ PERCENTAGE: ____ Characteristics: Concerns / Needs:

CONNECT!

The GRACE Pattern
for inviting a person to receive Jesus Christ as Lord and Savior

G God's grace for all

Scriptures for reflection:
- *Matthew 11:28-30*
- *Luke 15*
- *John 3:16-17*
- *Acts 10:36-43*

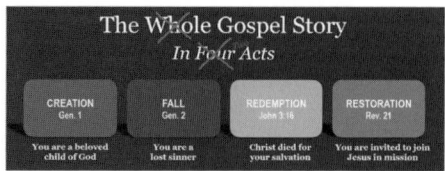

R Recognizing and Repenting of sin

Scriptures for reflection:
- *Psalm 51*
- *Mark 1:15*
- *Romans 3:9-18, 23, 4:4-5; 6:23; 7:18,24*
- *Ephesians 2:8-9*

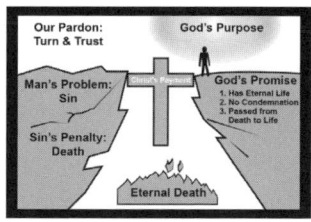

A Accepting God's forgiveness

Scriptures for reflection:
- *Matthew 26:28*
- *Acts 4:14; 16:29-31*
- *Romans 5:1*
- *Philippians 2:5-11*

First John1:9
"If we confess our sins, He is faithful and just to forgive us our sins and to cleanse us from all unrighteousness."

C Confessing faith in Jesus Christ

Scriptures for reflection:
- *Luke 15:17-20*
- *Romans 10:9*
- *Philippians 2:11*
- *Revelation 3:20*

E Engaging in life as a Disciple of Jesus

Scriptures for reflection:
- *Luke 22:14-23*
- *John 3:1-16*
- *Ephesians 4:7-16*
- *Romans 1:6*

CONNECT!

Love Your Neighbor Exercise

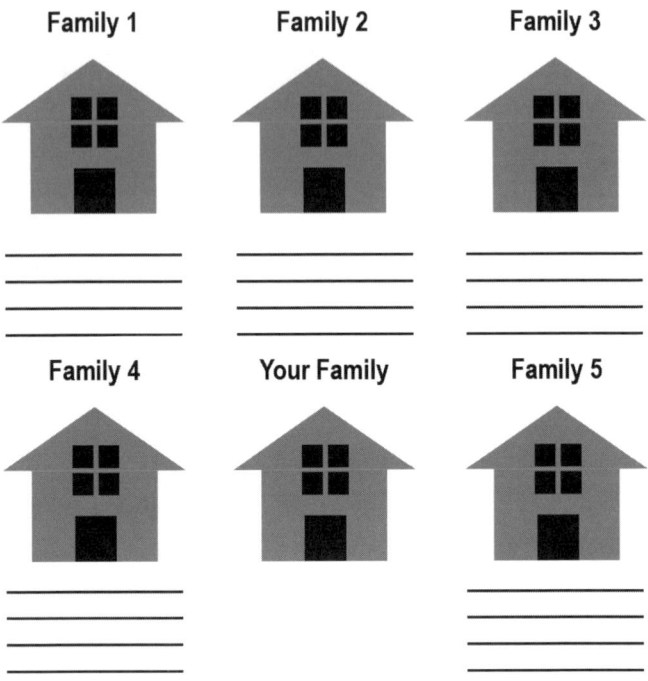

- Can you address all family members by name?
- Do you know what the career(s) are of the parent(s)?
- Have you been in each others homes? Had a real conversation?
- Have you shared a meal with that family?

How many of the families were you able to respond 'yes' to all questions for?

What does this say about your 'love of neighbor'?

Prayer Walking with Your Community
By Cheri R. Holdridge

An Introduction: WHY DO WE WALK AND PRAY?

Prayer is a precious gift. When we pray, we trust that God wants to communicate with us. When we pray, we open our side of communication with God. Because, you see, as every college freshman learns in Introduction to Speech class, communication takes two individuals, a speaker and a listener. In prayer, God always stands ready to listen. When we pray, we usually speak and we expect God to listen. In my own experiences of prayer, I find that prayer is deeper when I listen and wait for God to speak.

When we decide to "Prayer Walk" as individuals or as communities of faith, we are seeking to connect in a deeper way with the communities in which we live and we are inviting God to speak to us. We are asking God to show us what we have failed to see. We are asking God to give us new eyes to see what has become invisible to us over time, and new ears to hear what has become "white noise" to us.

The act of walking gives our bodies something to do. The walking is a sort of calming distraction so that our minds and our souls can focus on listening to God.

Prayer walking has been one of the most amazing adventures of my life as a pastor and as a Jesus follower. I offer this prayer guide to you as an invitation. I hope it will help you listen for God, and see God more intimately in your communities.

PRAYER WALK ONE

You probably have picked up this guide because you and some of your friends or fellow church members want to connect in a deeper way to your neighborhood or community. The practice of Prayer Walking is just that: a practice. There really are no rules. What I can offer you are the suggestions of a seasoned pastor who has done her share of walking and praying and trying to discern God's call.

The first two tasks are to gather a group of people who want to go on a Prayer Walk and decide where you will take your Prayer Walk. If you are part of an existing church, and you want to connect in a fresh way with your neighbors, I suggest you lay out a plan to walk in a radius of a few blocks of your church building. If you are investigating an area for a church plant or a site for expansion ministry, then pick a location for your Prayer Walk where you want to explore opportunities for ministry. Again, lay out a plan to walk a few blocks in this neighborhood. If there is a school, neighborhood center, or other community gathering place nearby, include that place in your walk. If there are both residential and commercial streets near your church or mission area, try to include some of both in your Prayer Walks.

Hopefully you will have more than one Prayer Walk Team. A team will consist of two or three people. Have each team walk a different route, or if you walk the same routes, stagger your start times so that you are not clumped together. We do not want to overwhelm our neighbors with too many strangers gawking at them. Someone (a pastor, leader of your study process, or other person) should plan in advance what the routes will be, and prepare a simple map for each Prayer Walk Team. In planning the routes, remember that many of your folks may have been driving to your church for years, but perhaps never have walked even one block in the neighborhood. (This fact in itself is telling.) So a map is essential. If you are in an inner city neighborhood, you may need to think about teaming people who are more comfortable in the city with people who are less comfortable walking in the city. Of course, walking in the daytime is probably better for everyone's comfort level in an unfamiliar place. When you have gathered your Prayer Walk Team of two or three people, sit down together and read through these questions. It will be better if you can put these pages aside during your walk and just take in the experience. It is fine if you need to jot down a few key notes to help you remember, but try not to walk around the neighborhood with a clipboard, like you are taking a survey. Relax, and be ready to open your eyes and ears, to pray and soak up the experience with all of your senses.

For this first Prayer Walk we simply want to see our neighborhood with fresh eyes. We are on an expedition, a journey to learn as much as we can about the environment surrounding our church facility as we open our eyes and our hearts to our neighbors. We want to observe everything we can about our community, so we can begin to get to know these strangers whose 'hood we visit every Sunday. Here are some things to look for:

1. What do the homes look like? What do you see in the yards and in the driveways? On the porches? Do they have driveways and porches? Is there landscaping? If so, what kind and how is it cared for?

2. What do the cars look like? Are they old or new? What makes and models are they? What kinds of bumper stickers do you see?

3. What people do you see and what evidence do you see of people? Are there children in this neighborhood? Bikes and toys? Are there senior citizens? People who like to garden or work on their cars? What race and possible nationality might the people be? Do you see any flags flying that give you signs of any ethnic heritage or any geographic background such as being from some particular part of the U.S or from other countries?

4. What businesses are in the neighborhood? Are they thriving? Or not?

5. Are there boarded up houses or houses for sale? Businesses for

sale or closed?

6. Are there any agencies serving this community? Any other churches? Schools?

Obviously I don't expect anyone to respond to all of these questions on any single prayer walk. I suggest you read through this list of questions a couple of times before you go on your walk, just to give you some ideas of the breadth of things to watch for.

Then, as you begin your walk simply pray this prayer: ***"God show me what you want me to see in this neighborhood."*** And start walking and watching.

Before you begin, agree on the amount of time you will walk, perhaps 15, 20, or 30 minutes. Try not to talk to the other people with whom you are walking during your walk. This is a time to watch and listen. What does God show you about your neighborhood? Is God nudging you? Are you seeing something you have never seen before in all the years you have been driving to your church in this place? What does that tell you? Try not to jump too quickly to conclusions or potential ministry ideas. We are not looking for solutions today. We are simply looking for clues and opportunities to connect with our neighbors.

At the end of your walk, meet with all the Prayer Walk Teams to process your experience. You might meet back at your church. Or if there is a coffee house or restaurant nearby, you might want to meet there for your conversation.

GROUP CONVERSATION ABOUT THE PRAYER WALK

When all the groups have gathered, **begin with a prayer**. Pray your own or use this suggested prayer to open your conversation.

Holy One, just as you walked with us today in our neighborhood, will You be with us now in our conversation? Give us clear heads to listen and learn from the observations of one another. God, you have given us *this neighborhood* as our location for ministry. We want to connect with our neighbors. Help us to see and hear what *YOU* want us to see and hear. Bless our conversation now and guide us by Your Spirit. Amen.

Next, have a facilitator lead everyone through a discussion of any or all of these questions.

1. What did you see that you expected to see, and what did you see that surprised you? Start by talking about anything *except* the people you saw. (This question in itself could take plenty of time to discuss. As the facilitator, try to keep people focused on the facts of what they saw, rather than jumping to conclusions and assumptions. Avoid moving ahead to "ministry ideas." Linger in the realm of observation.)

2. Next focus on the people: Who did you see? Who lives in our neighborhood? What do they look like? How are they like us, in physical appearance, and how are they different?

3. Did you smell, touch, taste, or hear anything worth noting?

4. Based on the facts of what we have seen today, what might we "guess" are the deepest needs and concerns of the people who live in their neighborhood? (Facilitator, remind the group that we do not know much about the people we observed, so at this point we just have some hunches. If we are going to be in ministry with people, in time, we will need to be in relationship with them and hear *them* speak about their wants and needs. For today, we are just tossing out some preliminary ideas based on what we do know.)

Close with prayer. Pray your own, or use this suggested prayer:

God of Creation, we thank you that you give us eyes to see and ears to hear new things. Forgive us that which we have failed to see and hear in the past. We regret that we have not always connected with our neighbors in all the ways we might have as a congregation. Today is a new day. We are thankful that you are a God of new beginnings. Fill us with your Spirit, O God. Breathe your new life into us. Give us strength and courage to see the ministry opportunities that you will lay in front of us in the coming days and weeks and months. For now, give us open hearts and minds; we ask these things in Jesus' name. Amen.

PRAYER WALK TWO

For your second Prayer Walk, you can walk the same route as the first, a week, two weeks, or a month later. The purpose of the second walk is to take our prayer and our reflection a bit deeper, so it is helpful if at least some of the participants also took part in the first Prayer Walk.

As with the first Prayer Walk, look over the questions a couple of times before you walk.

1. Pay close attention to the people you see on your walk. Make eye contact as you walk past them. Smile. Greet them with a "Hello" or a "Good Afternoon." You are a stranger in their neighborhood. Walkers for a stroll (and not for exercise) are rare these days. Let them know you are not a threat. If you have a chance, it's okay to introduce yourself and tell them you are from the church nearby and you are on a Prayer Walk. Don't spend too much time, but if you have a chance to let your neighbors know you are praying for them, by all means, do not miss this opportunity.

2. Consider how the people you see are similar or different from yourself and the people who attend your church. If these people walked into your church, would they "stick out?" And if so, how would they appear "different" from the people in your church? Think about all the various "categories" we use to break down groups of people. How do the people you

see in this neighborhood compare to the people who are part of your church in terms of the usual "categories": age, gender, race, class, education? (Of course, some of these things you cannot tell by walking down the street; you will be making assumptions, so be careful. But be aware that we often make assumptions when people walk into our churches. This is food for thought.)

3. Look at the types of clothes people are wearing, the kinds of houses they live in, and the cars they drive. Do they have tattoos? Are they clean-shaven? Do they wear designer suits? Do they appear to have showered recently? How is their hair cut? How is their personal "style" reflected in how they look? Would people in your church welcome them, or turn the other way, if they walked into your worship service? Why?

4. Are there signs in your neighborhood that people speak a language other than English? Does your church have a worship service in another language?

Some of these questions will be more relevant than others to your context. Read through this list of questions a couple of times before you go on your walk, just to have some ideas of the breadth of things to watch for.

Then, as you begin your walk simply pray this prayer or your own:

"God show us our neighbors with fresh eyes today. Open our hearts to the faces You want us to see. Amen."

Before you begin, agree on the amount of time you will walk, perhaps 15, 20, or 30 minutes. Try not to talk to the other people with whom you are walking during your walk. This is a time to watch and listen. Who is God showing you in your neighborhood? If you are planting a new church or ministry, this is a time to discern whether or not this is a place where your gifts are suited for ministry. We need to work where we can connect with people. Usually God does not call us to plant a new church in a place that is completely foreign to us. Most church planters are most successful in a place where they have some "affinity" with the community.

For those in an established church who are trying better to connect with their community, this is a time really to see our neighbors with fresh eyes. If we have become disconnected over the years with our neighborhood, this is the time to be honest and consider whether we can realistically connect with this neighborhood. If so, we need to take a close look at whom our neighbors are, and ask God to help us learn how to get to know them.

Finally, remember not to jump too quickly to conclusions or potential ministry ideas today. We are not looking for solutions yet. We are simply looking for clues and opportunities to connect with our neighbors.

At the end of your walk, meet with all the Prayer Walk Teams to process your experience. You might meet back at your church. Or if there is a coffee house or restaurant nearby, you might want to meet there for your conversation.

GROUP CONVERSATION ABOUT THE PRAYER WALK

When all the groups have gathered, **begin with a prayer**. Pray your own or use this suggested prayer to open your conversation.

> O God, give us gentle spirits as we share our experiences now. Guide us to see the people in our neighborhood through the eyes of Jesus. Give us wisdom to discern how we have missed opportunities to connect with our neighbors in the past. Give us courage to consider how we might reach out to our neighbors in new ways in the future. Most of all, give us open hearts to listen to you and to one another in this time of conversation today. Amen.

Next, have a facilitator lead everyone through a discussion of any or all of these questions.

1. Who did you see today, who could come to our church and fit in easily?

2. Now be brutally honest. Who did you see today that would really "stick out like a sore thumb" if they walked into our worship service?

3. What social barriers keep people from feeling "at home" when they come to our church?

4. Which of these barriers is it practical to think we could overcome? And which ones can we not overcome. (It's ok to recognize that our church cannot reach everyone. That's why there are many different churches.)

5. As a result of this prayer walk, is there any particular group of people that you are beginning to feel a "nudge" from God that your church might be being called to reach. These are people you are not currently reaching, but who live in your neighborhood. (This is a hunch at this point, a prayer "nudge" from God. We need to keep praying about this.)

6. Any other comments from today's Prayer Walk?

PRAYER WALK THREE (A SIMPLE ALTERNATIVE)

This Prayer Walk can be done after Prayer Walk One and Two, or in place of either of them. This simpler alternative to one of the first two Prayer Walks involves taking a walk around your neighborhood and observing your surroundings. Simply try to empty your heart and mind of any extraneous thoughts and feelings. Say a short prayer like this to God:

"God we want to be a church that cares for our neighborhood. Show us what You want us to see."

Go for a walk, and see what God shows you.

Then come back together and discuss your experience.

PRAYER WALK FOUR (A SITTING ALTERNATIVE)

If your church, or your church plant mission zone, is in a densely populated area, you might want to try choosing a location and just sitting and observing the people who walk by. This is also an option if you have persons for whom walking is not possible. Choose a park bench, or put some lawn chairs on the corner outside your church, and do the exercises listed in one of the Prayer Walks above.

NEXT STEPS AFTER THE PRAYER WALKS

Prayer walking is a spiritual practice that encourages us to open ourselves to God's leading, and to pay attention to our neighbors. Over time, many established churches lose touch with their physical neighbors. New churches, predictably, need to understand the mission context in which they want to plant a new ministry. Prayer walking is an amazing tool that allows us to open ourselves to see and hear and be led by God toward the ministry opportunities that God has in mind for us.

I encourage you in your Prayer Walks not to jump too quickly to ministry planning. We need to take time to listen and dream and to discern. Once we have done these things, when the time comes for some goal setting and strategic planning, I suggest a church be intentional about moving to this next step. Be clear that you are now moving from the "prayer and discernment" stage to the "ministry development stage." Of course, we pray all along the way, but we need to be clear about which stage we are in. This will help us not to move too quickly from the listening stage to the action stage.

When you are ready, move to the action stage, and develop a ministry plan around what you have learned from your Prayer Walks. Of course, you can return to Prayer Walking or continue Prayer Walking at regular intervals to strengthen your ministry along the way. Prayer is always a good practice!

In Conclusion: THE POWER OF PRAYER WALKING

I close with a personal word of encouragement. Some of my richest days of prayer walking started in the autumn of 2007. I was beginning to feel the nudge of God to wrap things up at the church where I had been pastor for many years. I had no idea at the time, but God was preparing me to take the leap of being a church planter. I took long prayer walks that September and October all over my neighborhood and the downtown area of Toledo Ohio.

Several times, I turned a corner and God said clearly to me: "No, not here. This place is toxic."

"No you can't hold on to this place anymore. It's time to let go and move on."

Then I began to walk in another part of the city. I began to dream dreams and see visions. By the spring, summer and fall of the next year my heart raced with visions of new ministry ideas for what would eventually become The Village Church. It took years before The Village Church would launch weekly worship and become the community it is today. Back in 2007 I had no clue. God could not show me The Village Church all at one time. I could never have comprehended it. I had to take that first step, and the next, and the next, while prayer walking with God. The Village Church is now a vital community of people, and most of them were not going to church anywhere before the Village became a church. The Village would not be a church, if another Jesus-follower had not encouraged me to try Prayer Walking. So now I am encouraging you to give it a try. In time, God's dreams will come true through you too. I'm sure of it. May God bless you, as you walk, pray, and listen for God's nudges for you.

Cheri R. Holdridge is a Church Planter and Pastor of The Village, a partnership of the United Church of Christ and United Methodist Church in Toledo, Ohio. The Village began weekly worship in 2009, but really started during Cheri's Prayer Walks in 2007. Cheri was ordained an elder in the West Ohio Conference, UMC in 1992. She is a graduate of Candler School of Theology in Atlanta, and grew up in Abilene, Texas. Cheri and her husband Kurt Young have two children: Rebecca and Jamie. Kurt and Cheri dream of a world for all children where diversity is celebrated and every child knows they are a beloved child of God.

END NOTES

CHAPTER ONE

1) Gary L. McIntosh, *What Every Pastor Should Know: 101 Indispensable Rules of Thumb for Leading Your Church.* Baker Books, 2013.

2) Simon Sinek, *Start with Why: How Great Leaders Inspire Everyone to Take Action.* Portfolio, 2009.

3) Paragraph 202, highlights added, T*he Book of Discipline of the United Methodist Church.* United Methodist Publishing House, 2012.

4) Bob Farr, Doug Anderson, Kay Kotan, *Get Their Name: Grow Your Church by Building New Relationships.* Abingdon Press, 2013.

5) http://whatis.techtarget.com/definition/millennials-millennial-generation

CHAPTER TWO

1) Stephen Sorenson, *Like Your Neighbor?: Doing Everyday Evangelism on Common Ground.* InterVarsity Press, 2005.

2) www.kristenschell.com

3) www.nextdoor.com

4) http://en.wikipedia.org/wiki/Missional_community

5) Alan Hirsch, *The Forgotten Ways Handbook.* Brazos Press, 2009, pp 92-94.

6) http://d3n8a8pro7vhmx.cloudfront.net/.

7) Alan Hirsch, *The Forgotten Ways Handbook.* Brazos Press, 2009, p 134.

8) Phil Maynard, *Shift: Helping Congregations Back into the Game of Effective Ministry.* Excellence in Ministry Coaching, 2013.

9) Bill Hybels and Mark Mittelberg, *Contagious Christian.* Zondervan, 1996.

10) Bill Hybels, *Just Walk Across the Room.* Zondervan, 2006.

11) Alan Hirsch, *The Forgotten Ways Handbook.* Brazos Press, 2009.

12) Stephen Sorenson, *Like Your Neighbor?: Doing Everyday Evangelism on Common Ground.* InterVarsity Press, 2005.

13) Bob Farr, Doug Anderson, Kay Kotan, *Get Their Name: Grow Your Church by Building New Relationships.* Abingdon Press, 2013.

CHAPTER THREE

1) David Kinnaman and Gabe Lyons, UnChristian. Baker Books, 2007.

2) Kit Yarrow, Decoding the New Consumer Mind: How and Why We Shop and Buy. Jossey-Bass, 2014.

3) Bob Farr, Doug Anderson, Kay Kotan, Get Their Name: Grow Your Church by Building New Relationships. Abingdon Press, 2013.

4) Alan Hirsch, The Forgotten Ways Handbook. Brazos Press, 2009.

5) Jim Ozier and Fiona Haworth, Clip-In: Risking Hospitality in Your Church. Abingdon Press, 2014.

6) Alan Hirsch, The Forgotten Ways Handbook. Brazos Press, 2009.

7) Alan Hirsch, *The Forgotten Ways Handbook*. Brazos Press, 2009.

8) http://wwwmystery/mysteryThinPlaces.html

9) http://www.stress.org/holmes-rahe-stress-inventory/

10) Doug Anderson and Michael Coyner, *The Race to Reach Out*. Abingdon Press, 2004.

CHAPTER FOUR

1) http://missioninsite.com/technology/sample-reports

2) http://www.pewforum.org/2015/05/12/chapter-1-the-changing-religiouscomposition-of-the-u-s

3) Alan Hirsch and Lance Ford, *Right Here Right Now*. Baker Books, 2011.

4) *The United Methodist Hymnal*. The United Methodist Publishing House, 1989.

5) Rick Rusaw and Eric Swanson, T*he Externally Focused Church*. Group, 2004.

6) Cheri Holdridge, Introduction to "Prayer Walking with Your Community" (see appendix).

7) Reggie McNeal, *Missional Renaissance: Changing the Scorecard for the Church*. Jossey-Bass, 2009.

8) Val Hastings, *Change Your Questions, Change Your Church*. Coaching4Clergy, 2012.

9) www.lifetreecafe.com

10) Christine Shinn Latona and Joe Daniels, *The Power of Real: Changing Lives, Changing Churches, Changing Communities*. Beacon of Light Resources, 2013.

11) Thomas G. Bandy, *See, Know & Serve The People Within Your Reach*. Abingdon Press, 2013.

CHAPTER FIVE

1) Henri Nouwen as quoted by Eric Cooter, "21st Century Wells: Christian Community in the Third Place," Ministry Matters, March 11, 2013, www.ministrymatters.com

2) Dino Rizzo, Servolution: *Starting a Church Revolution through Serving*. Zondervan, 2009.

3) Ibid.

4) Ibid.

5) Ibid.

6) Christine Shinn Latona and Joe Daniels, *The Power of Real: Changing Lives, Changing Churches, Changing Communities*. Beacon of Light Resources, 2013.

NOTES

Thurs Dec 19 — party for
        Foster Grandparents

decorate Center pieces
        - Trip - Busing cost.

Sept 29 - Play Bells

                    530
Bells - Next week Bells
        only - Oct 2

Oct 9 Next week no Practice
            practice Oct 16
        play - Oct 20

Oct 13 - go to Presbyterian
Church to play after
Church

        Sing 15, 22